# the new cottage

## INSPIRATION FOR AMERICA'S FAVORITE HOME

### KATIE HUTCHISON

The Taunton Press

The Taunton Press
Inspiration for hands-on living®

The Taunton Press, Inc., 63 South Main Street, PO Box 5506, Newtown, CT 06470-5506
Email:tp@taunton.com

Editors: Peter Chapman, Carolyn Mandarano
Copy Editor: Candace B. Levy
Cover design: Sandra Salamony
Interior design and layout: Sandra Salamony
Illustrator: Katie Hutchison

The following names/manufacturers appearing in *The New Cottage* are trademarks: Andersen®, Benjamin Moore®, Centor®, Drewexim®, Energy Star®, Formica®, Galvalume®, Glulam®, Haas Door®, HardiePlank®, Heat & Glo®, IKEA®, Jøtul®, Marvin®, Monopoly®, PaperStone®, Pratt & Lambert®, RAIS®, Regency®, Richlite®, Rubio®, Sheetrock®, Sherwin-Williams®, Styrofoam®, Thermax™, Weiland®, Wittus®

Library of Congress Cataloging-in-Publication Data

Names: Hutchison, Katie, author.
Title: The new cottage : inspiration for America's favorite home / Katie
  Hutchison.
Description: Newtown, CT : The Taunton Press, Inc., 2018.
Identifiers: LCCN 2018027403| ISBN 9781641550130 (hard cover) | ISBN
  9781641550147 (pbk.)
Subjects:  LSCH: Cottages--United States.
Classification: LCC NA7551 .H88 2018 | DDC 728/.370973--dc23
LC record available at https://lccn.loc.gov/2018027403

Printed in the United States of America
10 9 8 7 6 5 4 3 2 1

## DEDICATION

In memory of architect Geoff Koper,
a wise person, patient mentor, and good friend.

## ACKNOWLEDGMENTS

**A BOOK IS THE** result of people's belief in it. It takes a publishing team's belief, distributors' belief, as well as a writer's belief. And, in the case of a cottage design book, it also takes the belief of photographers and, perhaps foremost, the belief of homeowners in the cottages they create with the design and construction teams they engage. I am so very thankful to the many who believed in this project, contributed to it, and made it a reality.

I especially thank editor Peter Chapman, who I've now had the pleasure to work with on two books and who, as before, launched this book into motion. Many thanks to Carolyn Mandarano, Rosalind Loeb, and the rest of the Taunton team too. Special thanks to the cottage owners who generously shared their homes and stories with us and to the architects and designers who shared their design insight.

Most of all, thank you, Chris, my beloved husband, for believing in me and for finding us our sweet cottage to call home.

# CONTENTS

# INTRODUCTION: THE NEW COTTAGE

**FOR MANY A NEW ENGLANDER,** a Cape Cod cottage is the essence of "cottage." And so it was for my architectural mentor, Geoff Koper, who bought an antique Cape for himself; his wife, Lynn; and their menagerie of pets to enjoy in Barnstable, Mass. Sure, the kitchen was awkward, the front dormer windows were oddly proportioned, and an in-ground pool was devouring land better suited to a cottage garden. Nonetheless, thanks to Geoff's skills as an architect and Lynn's design savvy, they gradually transformed the Cape Cod cottage—now listed on the National Register of Historic Places—to suit today's living without sacrificing the inherent charm that attracted them to it in the first place.

The front of Geoff and Lynn's Cape Cod cottage peeks out from within the lush landscape that frames it. Its simple massing and 1½-story human scale lends the facade a friendly countenance.

The simple massing of the original half Cape and back ell, which still exists today, is captured in this old photo of the Koper's cottage, which dates back to 1840. Those are bedroom windows tucked under the sheltering roof. This photo predates the addition of a front porch that was later removed and the front dormer.

Geoff had years of experience managing complicated commercial and institutional projects as a partner in a large New York City architectural firm before moving with his wife to enjoy a quieter lifestyle on Martha's Vineyard (where he and I met working for an island residential architect) and then later deciding to launch his own architectural enterprise on the Cape (for which I freelanced as an architect). He and Lynn, a one-time home-accessories shopkeeper, both recognized—despite the interventions of previous home-owners—the design potential in the 1½-story cottage that would become their home.

Their renovations didn't involve changing the cottage's footprint or massing. "It's got a clarity about it," notes Lynn. Their inclination, instead, was to undo the consequences of modifications by others, so that the exterior would be more in keeping with a Cape Cod cottage of its c. 1840 vintage. To that end, they replaced small dormer windows with slightly taller six-lite over six-lite double-hung windows and intro-duced gardens in place of the pool. Inside, their improve-ments were discreet yet critical to creating the flow and access to daylight that helps their cottage feel fresh and updated. In an earlier rear addition by others, Geoff and Lynn recon-figured the galley kitchen, added a bay window, and opened the now brighter kitchen over a half-wall of bookshelves to the adjacent family room. New, light-gray granite and warm cherry accents in the kitchen and family room complement pale-gray original plaster walls and warm, antique wide-plank

pine floors. The dining space became more of a cozy alcove by simply removing the doors that led from it to the stairs, the kitchen, and the living area. Geoff and Lynn preserved the intimate scale of the front rooms, while slightly reconfig-uring them. The original, modestly sized front living room was reoriented to a new fireplace on an exterior wall sur-rounded by new custom built-ins. A full bathroom, previously accessed off the dining area, was redesigned to open onto the front first-floor bedroom. Window and door trim that is orig-inal and dressy in the front of the house becomes more and more simplified as you travel deeper into the house toward the more informal, newly renovated spaces.

Geoff and Lynn's vision converted a somewhat muddled Cape Cod cottage into a cottage for now. "We always liked a small, charming house with a nice outside garden . . . . It just makes me feel happy," says Lynn.

I don't doubt that Geoff and Lynn's affinity for cottages influenced mine. Geoff and I worked together updating and creating cottages for architectural clients in Martha's Vineyard and up and down the Cape. We agreed: The mere thought of "cottage" puts the mind at ease. A cottage is where life is simple, comforting, and true. Cottages are an informal, often hardy subset of small or smaller houses, gen-erally possessing a visceral grab on homeowners' imagina-tions. Cottages are a perennial favorite, thriving now, in part, because of the back-to-basics movement that's been gaining ground since the 2008 recession. The basics are evolving to include an updated take on the classic cottage—one that suits living today. In the face of technology's expanding scope and speed, and the resulting nearly ubiquitous reach of social media, the cottage now appeals to our increasing need to balance the virtual and the real, transience and durability, togetherness and solitude, the high-tech and the home spun. Now's the time to explore cottages anew.

My definition of *cottage* is fairly broad. For me, there are certain qualities that cottages share, no matter the location. For one, cottages are small. The 25 featured cottage dwellings within these pages range in size from 545 sq. ft. to 2,742 sq. ft., with the majority coming in around 1,400 sq. ft. The cottages from across North America exemplify 10 characteristics of captivating cottages. The characteristics aren't meant to be prescriptive but rather qualitative, leaving room for them to be successfully interpreted to accommodate different cottage tastes and contexts. You'll find visual icons that represent the 10 cottage characteristics throughout the book too. The case studies are organized by location type: near the water, in a field or wilderness, or part of a community. They include new construction and renovation/additions. They also represent a stylistic range.

In the back of the book, you'll find a bonus chapter of cottage retreats. The retreats are studios, pool houses, and getaways that capture many of the same cottage characteristics, often in an even smaller scale. So grab a cup of coffee, settle into a comfortable chair, and let's head to the cottage where we can kick back, breathe deeply, and be at home.

## WHAT IS A COTTAGE, AND HOW DOES IT DIFFER FROM A CABIN?

According to the Online Etymology Dictionary, the word *cottage* may stem from the Old Norse *kot*, which translates as "hut." Ever since I began working on this book, I've had fun asking people how they define a cottage. For some, a cottage is a vacation house. For others, it's a small dwelling near the water. Many describe a romantic British idea of a cottage: one that is made of stone with a whimsical storybook quality. Oh, and gardens—cottages have gardens, don't they? Some folks get a faraway look in their eye and offer that a cottage is a dreamy place. Well, it is. It's all those things and more.

The garden shed picks up on the economical use of white-cedar exterior shingles that appear on three sides of the main cottage but not the front. They've mostly weathered a soft, natural gray, suited to the hardy Cape Cod environment. The shed, which Lynn plans to convert into a garden retreat, helps define the edge of an outdoor room.

Historically, cottages took many forms. In eighteenth-century America, the boxy, steeply gabled Cape Cod cottage clad in readily available wood shingles—often from head to toe—punctuated with small divided-lite windows began to populate the colonies. Gothic Revival cottages, which expanded on the simple gabled box and frequently included cross gables and adornments like rafter tails, bargeboards, and fretwork on applied porches and balconies, caught on in the middle to late nineteenth century on the East and West Coasts. Around the same time, down South, Victorian detailing applied to deep, yet narrow, single-room-width dwellings, often with tall windows, resulted in the Shotgun style cottages prevalent in New Orleans. At the turn of the century and beyond, the Arts and Crafts bungalow became a popular, sturdy, 1½-story dormered cottage style with robust detailing. And then came the ubiquitous American Ranch style dwelling, a lower slung cottage often with a more open plan, wider windows, and greater length or wings that sometimes shape courtyards and patios. So a cottage isn't just one specific style; it encompasses many styles.

My anecdotal cottage polling also touched on how folks distinguish a cottage from a cabin. Most were fairly confident that a cabin is typically found in the woods. Possibly. But there are also cottages in the woods. When prodded further, some conceded that a cabin could also be found by the water. As could a cottage. I think you're unlikely to find many cabins in town or in a community, but you can certainly find cottages in town and in communities. Cabins seem to be associated a bit more with rugged, hard-scrabble individualism. Beyond that, cabins tend to evoke a rough-hewn construction style with lots of exposed natural or clear-finished wood inside and out. Cottages on the other hand, while also informal, tend to be a little crisper, often with painted or stained finishes inside and out. Cottages are less rustic than cabins and, dare I say, generally a bit more focused on togetherness—both with their natural environment and (when in less remote locations) with their neighbors.

Perhaps the best way to define a cottage for today is with the 10 characteristics of captivating cottages that I describe in the following pages. They should point you in the right direction.

The front living room includes a new fireplace, new crafted built-in shelving, and new high awning windows to welcome daylight from a second direction. Ernesto, the cat, appreciates the cozy, sunny spot.

New windows above the couch in the back ell add daylight while maintaining privacy from neighbors. The new bay window beyond brightens the work area in the galley kitchen. New custom cherry built-ins facing the family area add function, while a soffit above—of the same material—contributes to the refinement of the intersecting informal spaces.

The dining area is better integrated with the spaces around it due to the removal of the door to the stairs and other doors off the space, making it more alcove-like. The transom window above the stair doorway is an original detail that allows daylight to be shared from above as well as below and helps the steep, narrow stairs feel less cramped.

## 10 DESIGN CHARACTERISTICS OF TODAY'S COTTAGES

When we set out to select the cottages for this book, I knew I wanted them to speak to our moment now, while honoring the essence or spirit of our collective understanding of cottages. I cast a wide net, asking those interested to submit smaller dwellings that were either newly constructed or newly renovated and seemed like cottages to them. The challenge then became sorting the submissions based on more than a gut feeling of what seemed cottagey. I had drafted an early version of the 10 characteristics of new cottages—which I later developed into the definitions that follow—and found I returned repeatedly to my draft to test which submissions would qualify as a cottage. While I knew I was seeking variety in style and geography, I was also aiming to create a collection of cottages that would share a consistent framework of qualities. I then tweaked the framework as the collection took shape, and I observed with fresh eyes some characteristics the selections shared.

The 10 characteristics appear in the order you might consider them when first contemplating a cottage project: from initial site considerations to construction details. Your project might emphasize some of these characteristics more than others, depending on your proclivities and priorities. They aren't intended to be rules for how a cottage should look but more of a guide for making design decisions that contribute to creating a home that feels like a captivating cottage.

## THE ICONS

After proving a useful tool in my book *The New Small House,* the icons are back. They're small symbols that serve as a visual shorthand of sorts. Each represents a cottage characteristic. Look for the icons in the photo captions and project headers as a reminder of which characteristics are portrayed where. After spotting the icons in a few of the case studies, you may find that the various characteristics become easier to remember and, accordingly, easier to apply to your own cottage project in a location of your choosing.

 1. Engage with site

 2. Demonstrate human scale

 3. Communicate simple massing

 4. Provide a sheltering roof

 5. Convey an economy of means

 6. Offer informality

 7. Invite a sunny disposition

 8. Consider opposite complements

 9. Celebrate wabi sabi

 10. Shape crafted details

 ENGAGED WITH SITE: The cottage addition off the back of this renovated barn in Maine steps down into the landscape as do a variety of stone terraces that ease the transition from enclosed dwelling to engaged southern meadow. (Design by Whitten Architects; see also pp. 124–131.)

HUMAN SCALE: Intimate environments such as this front porch in Rhode Island, featuring a swinging bench beneath small awning windows, comfortably relate to our human scale while remaining airy. (Design by Katie Hutchison Studio; see also pp. 148–154.)

## 1 ENGAGED WITH SITE

A hallmark of a cottage has long been how it's integrated with the landscape. Think of Norwegian folk cottages that seem to grow out of the landscape with sod roofs and organic stone walls or English cottages surrounded by picturesque eddies of wildflowers, fragrant herbs, and swaying shrubs. Today's cottages may likewise be nested within compact and boisterous flower beds, or they may be integrated more subtly among tall cedars and pines, snug to a rock outcrop or perched above a nearby body of water. Their footprints might be minimized for low impact on the environment, or they may be shaped in response to site features, bumping out to catch a view or stepping back to preserve space for outdoor living. If a new cottage is located within a community, it might engage with the context via its placement in relation to its neighbors, thus shaping outdoor rooms, and/or it might engage with the context via something as simple as a porch.

## 2 HUMAN SCALE

*Scale* is a relative term. It's different from size, which doesn't include a reference. For example, how small is small? How large is large? It's difficult to say. But scale can be related to a specific unit. In the case of "human scale," a human is the unit. Stairs are a great example of something designed to the human scale. A step height and depth is meant to be comfortably managed by our climbing stride. So a dwelling like a cottage that's built with human scale in mind is designed to take into consideration how people move through space, use space, and perceive space relative to themselves. A cottage may relate to human scale by having eaves that aren't too terribly far overhead, so the cottage doesn't feel towering but approachable. It might feature a plan in which spaces comfortably accommodate typical human walking patterns and furniture groupings that seat a small gathering rather than spaces large enough for a pride of lions to roam, for example. Material arrangement might similarly relate to human scale, so board widths and tile dimensions are no larger than what can be carried and placed by human hands. Human scale now is pretty much as human scale before, though perhaps humans now have grown accustom to a little more breathing room both between and above them, which results in slightly airier cottage spaces.

 **SIMPLE MASSING:** Uncomplicated forms like these two gable wings in Washington create a simple, legible composition that reaches toward those arriving to funnel them in between into the entry; one wing contains living spaces and the other accommodates sleeping spaces. (Design by Prentiss + Balance + Wickline Architects; see also pp. 112–117.)

## 3 SIMPLE MASSING

 The form and volume of a structure contribute to its massing. If you imagine a Monopoly house or hotel, you're imagining simple massing. The Monopoly house is essentially a cube with a gable roof, a simple mass. The Monopoly hotel is a rectangular cuboid with a gable roof, another simple mass. These are forms that are easy to wrap your head around and understand. Such should be the case with a cottage. This doesn't mean that these simple forms can't be combined to create new forms or that the roofs must be gables, but in order for the forms to remain simple to understand, the complexity of their massing should be minimal. Ideally a cottage's massing communicates its use and/or the hierarchy of its use. A larger volume might contain a shared living space; a smaller volume might suggest an ancillary space like a bedroom or an entry porch. Every roof element or footprint jog should be purposeful, not busy. This makes a cottage legible and relatable. Today's cottages are often pared down.

## 4 SHELTERING ROOF

The crux of a cottage is the idea of shelter. It's a place where we feel protected, secure, even cozy. The roof is critical in creating shelter. A roof that can be occupied is sheltering. It might be occupied by living spaces snug beneath its eaves and perhaps accommodated within dormers. Or it might be occupied in the sense that its slope forms an engaging positive space even well below it. A roof with extended overhangs can increase a cottage's sense of shelter. It needn't be a certain type of roof to provide a sheltering presence. It could be a gable, shed, mansard, gambrel, hipped, or—yes—flat roof (that's to scale). Attention to roofing material and eave and rake details can help accentuate the roof and the brim it provides to ward off inclement weather, offer shade, and comfort us. A design that emphasizes and occupies the roof highlights its capacity for shelter and can lend a cottage vibe.

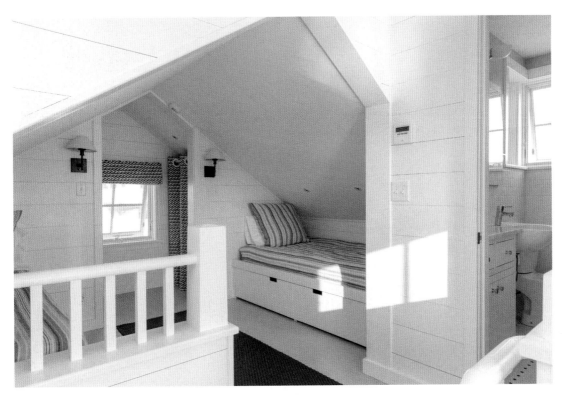

 SHELTERING ROOF: Spaces that occupy a sloping roof like this third-floor bedroom in this beach cottage feel cozy, protected, and sheltered. (Design by Whitten Architects; see also pp. 18–26.)

## 5 ECONOMY OF MEANS

There's an inherent simplicity to a cottage, and that simplicity extends not only to its massing but to the materials that compose it. Simple materials simply assembled, like painted, exposed studs and board sheathing, represent an economy of means you might find in a cottage. Painted, broad, interior shiplap cladding on walls and ceilings alike might represent a more modern economy of means in a new cottage. In such cases, material choices and their assembly are straightforward and uncomplicated. Whether the structure is exposed or concealed, a cottage for today generally has a no-nonsense attitude toward finishes chosen from a small or limited palette of materials and colors, which helps tie spaces together and yields a calm, more spacious effect. An economy of means may also translate to a limited use of financial resources. That, of course, may depend, in part, on the selected palette of materials.

 ECONOMY OF MEANS: A concise palette of material and colors in this Wolfe Island cottage in Ontario, Canada, has a serene and refined effect. (Design by superkül; see also pp. 27–33.)

 INFORMALITY: Opening the generous kitchen to the dining/living area beyond and the back patio to the left in this Del Mar, Calif., cottage creates an informal flow in which entertaining and food prep overlap as do the indoors and outdoors. (Design by Nick Noyes Architecture; see also pp. 48–55.)

## 6 INFORMALITY

 Cottages of yore, which often contained small somewhat formal rooms with smallish windows, could feel somewhat dark and cramped. Cottages now tend to have more open plans, larger windows, and different patterns of use than their more formal predecessors. Dining rooms have become dining alcoves or share space with living areas and kitchens. The front closet might have

morphed into a peg rail in a walk-through mudroom. The entrance off a modest vestibule might be straight into a kitchen/family space rather than a more conventional living room. An outdoor shower might connect directly to a bathroom or bedroom. Informality can also extend to finishes, fixtures, and furnishings that aren't fussy or demanding. Informality can contribute to an understated cottage for today.

 SUNNY DISPOSITION: Ganged large windows that extend nearly floor to ceiling in the faceted wall of this waterfront cottage in Scarborough, Maine, brighten the living area and invite the panoramic view indoors. (Design by Winkelman Architecture; see also pp. 69–75.)

## 7 SUNNY DISPOSITION

Older cottages generally had smaller windows due to concern about potential heat loss and the expense associated with the limited availability of large glass panes. But thanks to today's improved window and glass-door engineering, high-performance building envelopes, and interior climate control, larger windows and glass doors are readily available and often ganged to create even larger openings without sacrificing thermal comfort. Spaces washed with daylight warm us physically and emotionally. An enticing window seat, a bright breakfast nook, or a dormer-lit arm chair—complete with a cat sunning itself—brim with cottage cheer. Daylight spaces draw us toward them and enliven and enlarge adjacent spaces that are open or visually connected to them. Cottages invite daylight through a variety of openings, such as windows of many sizes, glazed doors, slatted screens, clerestory windows, skylights, and roof monitors. They invite daylight to travel deep within thanks to more open plans, aligned doorways, partial-height walls, cathedral ceilings, and interior windows/transoms. Interior color selections and finish patterns may also amplify a sense of sunniness. A sunny cottage courts contentment.

## 8 OPPOSITE COMPLEMENTS

The variety of spatial experiences you might encounter in a larger house when moving through a number of additional spaces needs to be expressed more concisely in a smaller cottage. The use of nearby contrast in the form of opposite complements makes this possible in captivating cottages. For example, to appreciate a more intimate space, you need a proximate contrasting taller or more public space. The intimate space and the taller/public space are opposite but complement each other in the sense that they enhance each other much the same way that opposite colors complement each other. The same type of contrast or opposite complements could apply to finishes and shapes, like having a smooth finish paired with a rough one or an organic shape juxtaposed against something orthogonal. These types of local or nearby contrasts add nuance and enrich the experience of today's cottages.

 OPPOSITE COMPLEMENTS: The snug sleeping nook and the taller multipurpose living/dining/kitchen space it adjoins in this Foster, R.I., cottage offer contrasting spatial qualities that are each enhanced by their proximity to the other. (Design by 3SIXØ Architecture; see also pp. 106–111.)

## 9 WABI SABI

The meaning of *wabi sabi*—a tradition in the Japanese aesthetic—has evolved. It's come to be understood as the beauty inherent in impermanence. That beauty may reveal itself in a patina or weathered finish on the cottage itself, in rustic furnishings within the cottage that divulge their history, or even in cottage housewares like a fractured bowl that celebrates the patch where it was fractured. Or it may be evident in a framed view of a natural, seasonal, changing scene. A cottage designed for today embraces wabi sabi perhaps, in part, because it underscores the informality of cottages and their place in a real and ever-evolving natural environment in which impermanence is part of the natural cycle.

 WABI SABI: Aged hemlock floors add depth, color, and texture to the newly renovated cottage in the Oak Bluffs community of the Martha's Vineyard Campground. Weathered and distressed furniture similarly reflect wabi sabi charm. (Design by Erin Cummings; see also pp. 162–167.)

 CRAFTED DETAILS: Overhanging rake trim crafted of three boards layered atop each other adds depth, shadow, and interest to this informal board-and-batten cottage in a Washington pocket neighborhood. (Design by Ross Chapin Architects; see also pp. 174–181.)

## 10 CRAFTED DETAILS

Attention to how materials are shaped and joined is a hallmark of cottages. Historically, those details were hand crafted. Cottages today also celebrate crafted details, created by hand or with the help of more modern tools and equipment. Designing the connection of one material to another, the transition from one plane to another, or how an element terminates or extends is an architect's joy. Even a material selection itself can communicate craft in that its use as a finish in a particular application is unusual or imaginative. Whether the material selection is crafted or the details are made in a more traditional fashion or a more modern manner, the thoughtful, refined resolution of intersections, transitions, and treatments can communicate cottage.

Part of the fun of living in a cottage or visiting one on a regular basis, is that its cottageness is ever evolving. Shells collected last season find a home along the screen porch rail;

a small cottage portrait discovered at a flea market gets added to the half bath; another planting bed for rhubarb is dug to round out the garden. You may find that your cottage design evolves too. Whether your cottage project is a renovation/addition or new construction, some of the cottage characteristics described here may speak to you at different moments in the design process and over time. Because they overlap and interrelate, one characteristic may inspire how you interpret another.

Geoff and Lynn Koper's cottage continues to evolve. Lynn has plans to turn the backyard tool shed into an outdoor cottage retreat for entertaining. She'll have a chance to consider all of the cottage characteristics afresh as she shapes her cottage's Mini-Me.

Sample how the 10 cottage characteristics are expressed in the case studies that follow to gain a better understanding of how they can be interpreted to shape unique cottages for today. This will help you imagine or create your own dwelling that captures the inimitable appeal of the new cottage.

# BY THE WATER

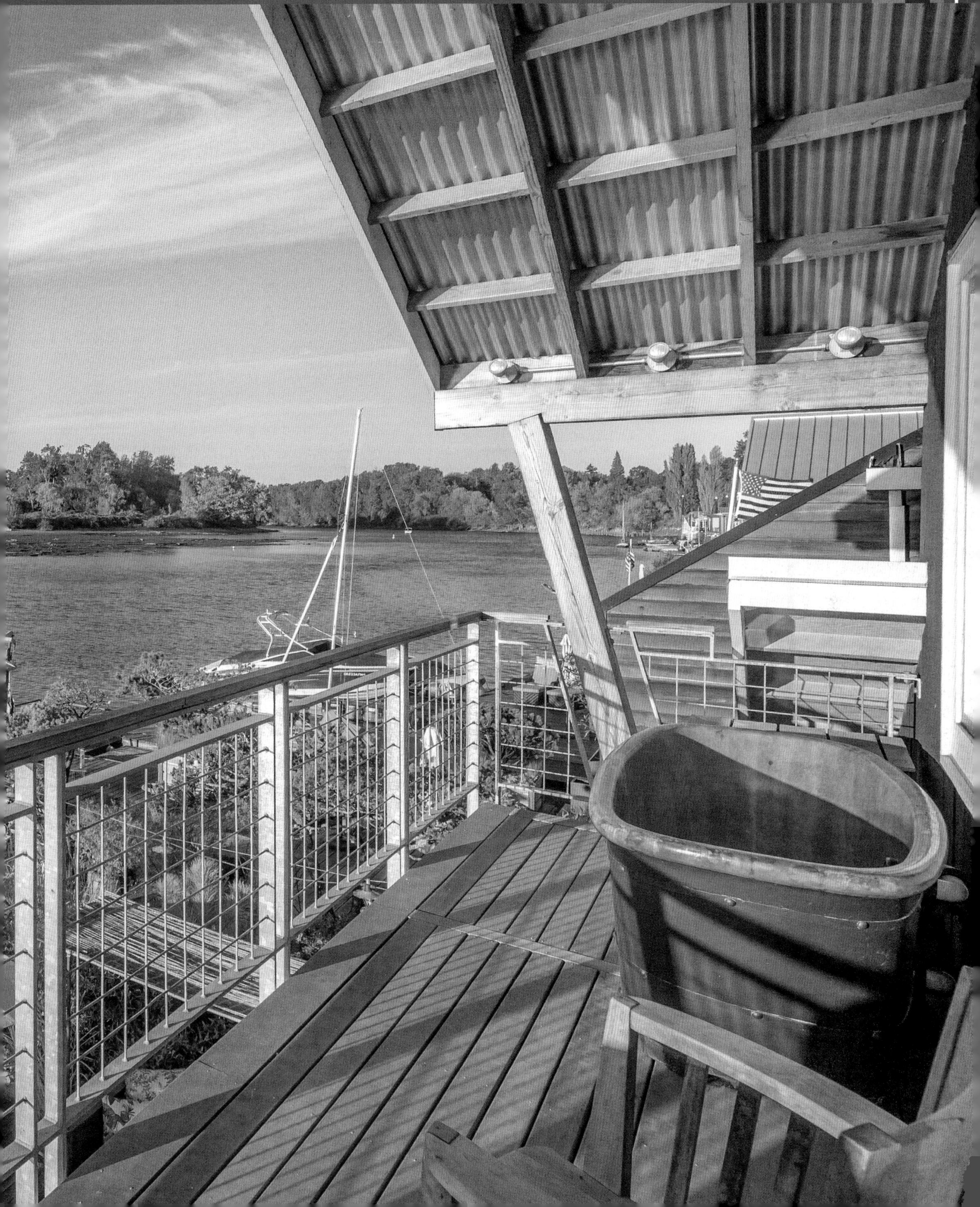

# BEACHFRONT DUO

ENGAGED WITH SITE

HUMAN SCALE

SIMPLE MASSING

SHELTERING ROOF

ECONOMY OF MEANS

INFORMALITY

SUNNY DISPOSITION

OPPOSITE COMPLEMENTS

WABI SABI

CRAFTED DETAIL

**SOMETIMES THE PROJECTS WITH THE MOST STRINGENT RESTRICTIONS** result in the most interesting and satisfying results. Such is the case with this property owned by the Seaver family in the densely sited Higgins Beach village of Scarborough, Maine. Consisting of two existing buildings on a mere 5,000-sq.-ft. lot, it was subject to tight building restrictions from the town, state, and Maine Department of Environmental Protection (DEP). Working deftly and patiently within the restrictions and in conversation with the overseeing authorities, Rob Whitten and Russ Tyson of Whitten Architects transformed the two disparate structures into two integrated cottages for today.

The spirit of the place is a barefoot world.

Wrapped in white-cedar shingles with red-cedar vertical-board accents at the entry porches to both cottages and on the new third-floor dormers, the exterior materials, which will weather gray, speak to a hardy New England cottage tradition as do exposed, crafted rafter tails. Oversized corner window assemblies hint at a more contemporary cottage aesthetic as do the ultra-durable, standing-seam sheltering roofs. Native plants out front soften the height of the raised cottage and replace what had previously been a paved parking area.

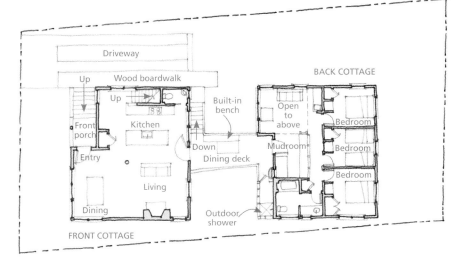

**Architect:** Whitten Architects: Rob Whitten, Principal, and Russ Tyson, Project Architect

**Decorator:** Hurlbutt Designs: Louise Hurlbutt and Ilyse Sandler

Scarborough, Maine

Front cottage: 1,555 sq. ft.
Back cottage: 895 sq. ft.
Total: 2,450 sq. ft.

FRONT COTTAGE SECOND LEVEL

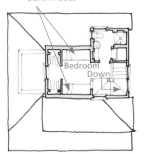
FRONT COTTAGE THIRD LEVEL

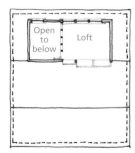
BACK COTTAGE SECOND LEVEL

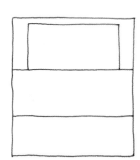
BACK COTTAGE ROOF

   Both the primary front cottage and accessory back cottage exhibit simple massing. The entry porch lends the front cottage human scale as do the asymmetrical dormers on both cottages, which favor the setback-conforming side of the property. Concrete piers tied to underground structural concrete pads, which prevent the cottages from washing out to sea in a flood, are lightly screened by 5/4 stock western red-cedar slats, designed to be pervious to sand and flood material.

New oversized windows capitalize on the view corridor off the dining area, creating a porch-like sunny space. The eaves dip at the corner to meet an existing condition and lend the space intimacy beneath the sheltering roof. White-oak floors, with a whitewash, driftwood-like Rubio Monocoat finish, run throughout the front cottage main level.

The living area, which is open to the dining and kitchen areas, takes advantage of the lower eaves line to incorporate built-ins, including a recessed cabinet over the fireplace for the TV. It's hidden behind custom bifold doors, made of the same vertical-board finish as the walls and adorned with a seascape mural of Higgins Beach by Kennebunk, Maine, artist Susan Amons.

A former summer community, Higgins Beach was originally populated with affordable dwellings including many that had been temporary housing for laborers during World War II and had been moved from the Portland and Scarborough areas to Higgins Beach afterward. Jeff and Jen Seaver, as well as the architects, suspect that the two buildings on the Seaver's lot were likely originally such cottages constructed in the 1940s, perhaps in the South Portland Shipyard area, that were later relocated to their current site. "The spirit of the place as a barefoot world, as a place where you relax, and a place where you go to be together," says Rob is what the Seavers wanted to capture in the renovated cottage. Having grown up vacationing on Higgins Beach as a kid for a week or two at a time in a family friend's cottage, Jeff saw the two cottages that he and Jen acquired as an opportunity to pass the tradition of carefree, beach living onto their two daughters. Since they were relocating from Chicago to London while the renovation was taking place and suspected there would be other moves in their future, Jeff and Jen also aspired for the renovated cottages to serve as a consistent, lasting home base for the family.

The open kitchen includes a white, vertical-board finish on the island that's narrower than the horizontal-board finish on the walls, which relates to the island's smaller, more furniture-like scale. Handmade fireclay tiles in the backsplash in a simple running bond pattern provide a burst of sea-inspired color and texture that the honed Norumbega granite counters pick up on.

The master bedroom boasts a great view through the ribbon of double-hung windows. A simple dividing muntin in the top window sash is a cottage touch, while the lower sash (which is open) is muntin-free for an unobstructed view when seated or in bed. The small balcony, set into the porch roof below, offers an intimate open-air roost that complements the large flat-ceilinged interior space of the bedroom.

When the Seavers acquired the property, which was considered nonconforming with respect to town zoning at the time, the two-story front cottage had already undergone a renovation by a previous owner in or around 2004, when it was converted to a year-round family residence that had resulted in, among other things, it being raised 3 ft. in accordance with a Maine DEP requirement. But the one-story back summer cottage was relatively untouched, still at the original lower level, with its own unrelated entrance, and in a state of disrepair.

In an effort to reduce some of the property's non-conformities and to improve the relationship between the two structures and the site, the architects moved the equivalent of the back cottage forward by approximately 6 ft. and raised it 3 ft. on piers to comply with DEP requirements. This put its first floor in alignment with the first floor of its sister cottage. It was constructed anew to match the footprint, human scale, and simple massing of the gable roof of the original, plus the addition of a small shed dormer above a new loft within the sheltering roof on the zoning-conforming side of the

 The consistent white, board finish on the walls and Monocoat whitewash finish on the white-oak floors allow the various blues and aquas of the furnishings, bedding, and artwork in the master bedroom to pop. "We like to bring the outside into the house: the exterior, the sea, the sky . . . ." says decorator Louise Hurlbutt.

Shipshape twin beds on the third floor of the front cottage nestle under the sheltering roof. The custom-built beds were designed with the Seavers' daughters in mind, though Jen's parents also like the top-floor perch for its view and generous full bath. Budget-friendly, painted pine floors in this space recall a traditional cottage finish. "It's both a contemporary look as well as one that has some precedence," says Rob.

property. They also converted it from an independent dwelling with its own full kitchen and dining space into a bunk house for guests and kids.

Though the DEP wouldn't permit an additional structure with a roof, like a screen porch or breezeway to connect the two cottages, they would allow an uncovered 200-sq.-ft. deck. So the architects ingeniously sited a dining deck bridge adjoining the two cottages, creating its own outdoor room within the overall outdoor room between the cottages, engaging the site. "It's kind of a fun design challenge; the farther apart you make the two pieces, the less [deck] width we're afforded. So how wide do you make it? How long do you

make it, and all stay under 200 sq. ft.?" asks Rob. They ended up angling the south edge of the deck plan a bit like the bow of a boat to make the math work, while allowing enough width to circulate past the deck dining table.

The front cottage, when the Seavers acquired it, lacked an entry porch. The architects rectified this by counterintuitively carving out interior conditioned space to craft a welcoming covered outdoor entry porch. As soon as you enter, your line of sight is directed right back out to the beach. "One of the things we feel really strongly, from a design perspective, is that you're here because there's this outside experience of the beach. We love creating a nice transition from inside

The deck dining bridge connecting the front cottage, which the Seavers have named "Sand Dollar," to the back cottage, named "Lobster Pound," is just wide enough to snuggly house a built-in bench and table with circulation space behind the dining chairs. A boat-like cable rail relates to the nautical theme expressed in both cottages.

to outside," notes Rob. The entry porch not only provides shelter while you're fumbling with keys but it's also a place to drop off your beach props.

What had been a jumble of first-floor rooms in the front cottage with little daylight or connection to the borrowed view of the ocean, the architects transformed into an open living area with new and larger windows throughout, positioned to capture daylight and the borrowed water view, creating sunnier, more expansive spaces better visually connected to the beach. "We like the great-room concept," says Jeff. It allows them more generous space for family and informal entertaining of larger groups. A new third floor, housed

within new dormers that complied with the significant zoning setback requirements, accommodates custom built-in twin beds under the sheltering roof, as well as an additional full bathroom.

Both cottages feature a calming backdrop of walls finished with wide tongue-and-groove boards painted white and installed horizontally, with gaps the thickness of a nickel between them, which contribute shadow lines and scale. "It's a finish that can move and expand and contract on a very exposed site with relationship to water and moisture," notes Russ. It's tough and durable and evokes an updated cottage aesthetic. Decorators Louise Hurlbutt and Ilyse Sandler

 Oversized windows flood the sitting area in the back cottage with sunlight. This cottage features the same wall and painted-floor finish as the third floor of the front cottage, but here additional height from the new dormer lends the small area greater spaciousness. A ladder provides playful access to the small loft that the Seaver daughters have nicknamed the "Lobster Fort."

brought their signature blue-and-white palette to the paint selections, furnishings, and textiles in both cottages, and reinforced the nautical look the architects hint at with, among other details, a mast-like post in the open living area that's comprised of white oak wrapping a steel column.

The renovated compound reflects updated beach-cottage living. "It's honoring the history but not copying it," notes Russ. "We made it so that every generation can enjoy it,"

says Jeff. Both his and Jen's parents visit along with extended family, and someday their daughters may bring their own families, too. "Part of the cottage tradition is that you shared a cottage, and they're all sharing it," says Rob. One of the great perks of the many building constraints on a small lot is the togetherness it affords.

# AGRICULTURAL VERNACULAR

ENGAGED WITH SITE · HUMAN SCALE · SIMPLE MASSING · SHELTERING ROOF · ECONOMY OF MEANS · INFORMALITY · SUNNY DISPOSITION · OPPOSITE COMPLEMENTS · WABI SABI · CRAFTED DETAIL

A modern cottage that belongs to the landscape.

**PETER SCHNEIDER AND RICHARD ALMONTE** sent their architect, Meg Graham, a principal at superkül, unusual photo inspirations for their new getaway on Wolfe Island, the largest of the Thousand Island archipelago in the St. Lawrence River, which spills into Lake Ontario. "We sent her all these pictures of crumbling barns, old abandoned farmhouses, an old schoolhouse, and we said, 'This is it; this is what we want our cottage to look like,' " says Peter, laughing. He and Richard had spent time getting familiar with the island and were drawn to the many and sundry agricultural buildings that populate it, which inspired them to ask Meg to design a modern cottage that similarly belongs to the landscape.

  The approach toward the crisp, shed-inspired, simple form sets the stage for a unique waterfront cottage engaged with its context. A slightly elevated beachy boardwalk flanked by billowing decorative grasses leads to an overscaled opening that offers a glimpse of the lake in the distance. The front door is under cover of the opening.

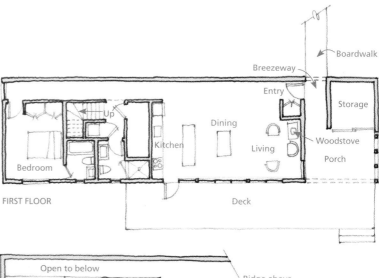

Boardwalk

Breezeway

Entry

Storage

Dining

Kitchen

Woodstove

Living

Bedroom

Porch

FIRST FLOOR

Deck

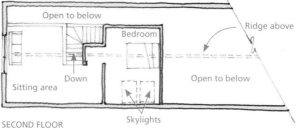

Open to below

Bedroom

Ridge above

Down

Sitting area

Open to below

Skylights

SECOND FLOOR

The informal cedar boardwalk and cedar walls (as well as the ceiling) of the porch/breezeway will gently weather gray, adding to the beachy effect. The horizontal installation of the breezeway/porch wall (and ceiling) finish foreshadows similar treatments inside.

**Architect:** superkül:
Meg Graham, Principal
Wolfe Island, Ont., Canada
1,250 sq. ft.

On the lake side, the cottage opens up with tall glass doors and windows as well as a tall covered porch/breezeway under the sheltering roof. A comfortably deep deck runs the whole length of the cottage at the same level as the interior floor, allowing each to visually borrow space from the other.

Meg's response is a long, narrow, shed-like form that runs northeast to southwest. She describes Wolfe Island as almost prairie-like and quite sublime. "In that context, this equally sublime and almost mute form of this agricultural building connects really well," she explains. Finished in durable, white, smooth HardiePlank lap siding and capped with a galvanized standing-seam, simple gable roof, the cottage presents a quiet, windowless long facade to the street for privacy. Yet it entices passersby with a 12-ft.-tall, scale-defying opening seemingly cut through the dwelling (toward the south end of its length) that frames a view of Lake Ontario beyond. A long, elevated human-scaled boardwalk, edged on both sides with decorative grasses, lightly engages the site as it proceeds perpendicular to the cottage, aligned with the opening through it, toward the front door. "It's a little magical to me," notes Meg. The boardwalk and grasses figuratively anticipate the beachfront to come (though Meg notes that the actual lakeshore is rocky).

 The cedar on the covered porch/breezeway provides a welcome textured contrast to the white finish outside and in. Crafted, oversized barn sliders, elegantly camouflaged to blend in, provide access to the shed storage. The slatted cedar on the south wall both filters light and provides some privacy from the neighbor.

The opposite long side of the cottage addresses the lake with 8-ft.-tall swaths of glass doors and windows, a deck, and a cedar-clad covered porch that backs up against a storage shed that Meg positioned so it shares the main roof and appears from the street like an extension of the house. The shed conveniently stores water toys and garden implements during the offseason, when Peter and Richard visit less frequently. Though the cottage is winterized, they use it primarily from May through October

Guests are given the second-floor bedroom, which is tucked under the sheltering roof along with a loft. Peter and Richard opted not to include dormers on the second floor, maintaining the cottage's uncomplicated form. Meg notes that such simple forms, "ultimately, are about practicality. They're about economy." She continues, "When I say *economical*, I mean structurally and expression-wise, but also very much from a cost perspective." To allow for adequate headroom upstairs within the simple form, the slope of the gable springs from several feet above the second floor. Large pivot-style skylights in the bedroom provide view, daylight, and ventilation, while gable-end windows do the same for the loft.

Beneath the sheltering roof, the horizontal reveals in the wall and ceiling finish lead the eye deep into the open living/dining/kitchen space and beyond. Peter's father, a retired tile setter, laid the grounding, Italian porcelain-ceramic floor tiles throughout the first-floor living spaces, as well as the smaller scale tiles in the bathrooms. "I just wanted something of my dad at the cottage," says Peter.

Tall windows and doors sun the space and provide visual connection and expansion to the outdoors. The kitchen island, finished on three sides with aspen white marble, is designed to appear like a solid block as a backdrop to the dining area. Peter imagined it as a substantial sugar cube. Overhead cabinets were deliberately omitted to downplay the kitchen.

   Bracketed by tall glass windows, the flexible living area includes a Regency woodstove sidled up next to the entry closet. The black flue stretching and jogging up and out is a playful contrasting accent as are the simple steel rod ties, allowing structure and infrastructure to act as ornament in this setting.

Inside, all-white, painted-poplar, tongue-and-groove boards, crafted with reveals, finish the walls and cathedral ceiling, picking up on the exterior aesthetic and then some. "When you walk in, there are these endless long, horizontal lines that lead to kind of a tranquility and peacefulness," says Richard. Though the cottage's footprint is small, Peter and Richard appreciated that the tall volume of the informal living/dining/kitchen would feel even more expansive with a succinct, linear palette, expressing an economy of means. That thinking extends to the kitchen work area, where they omitted kitcheny overhead cabinets in lieu of a simple crafted recess, accented by a streamlined stainless-steel hood and its ducting. A nearby teak sideboard supplements their kitchen storage needs. "The last thing I wanted was everyone who walks in to think, 'I'm in a kitchen,'" Richard notes. "I want a kitchen in the living room; I don't want it to feel like the living room is in the kitchen," adds Peter.

Rather than focus on the kitchen or living room, folks might focus instead on the view outside, thanks to the ganged tall glass doors and windows facing the deck and lake view. Daylight streaming in bounces light off the white walls and ceiling and draws you toward the outdoors. A tall window at the end of the hall that extends beyond the kitchen area has a similar effect, drawing you toward it to explore what happens beyond. "You really don't know where the house ends," says Peter, who appreciates the mystery of the cottage gradually revealing itself. The hall leads first to stairs, a laundry closet, and a full bath. At the very end is the master bedroom, in the most private location.

When Peter and Richard aren't on the island, they lead busy city lives in Toronto, so they relish returning to the cottage. "It's an antidote to the hectic pace of big-city living . . . given how busy and frenetic life is now," says Richard. "It's designed for easy living," he notes. Much of their time is spent on the covered porch or deck, sharing meals and drying off from a swim. "It's about spending time breathing, watching the trees move, watching the water come to the shore . . . . It doesn't have to be big," muses Meg.

The window at the end of the hall of horizontal lines entices, as does the light washing down from the loft above. "We love the grandness of that hallway," says Meg, "especially in such a small cottage."

The more intimate scale of the loft, under the sheltering roof, complements the double-height space below. The play of full-height planes defining the enclosed bedroom and half-height walls bordering the hall below animates the space. An exposed steel pipe column provides honest purpose and visual accent, like the handrail and other elements seen downstairs.

 The guest bedroom, under the sheltering roof, enjoys daylight and ventilation from large pivoting skylights. The whimsical scrolled headboard and old trunk are typical of the warm and inviting furnishings Peter and Richard chose to play off the crisp white interior. "Pretty much everything in there is vintage and antique," explains Peter.

# AN UPDATED CLASSIC

ENGAGED WITH SITE    HUMAN SCALE    SIMPLE MASSING    SHELTERING ROOF    ECONOMY OF MEANS    INFORMALITY    SUNNY DISPOSITION    OPPOSITE COMPLEMENTS    WABI SABI    CRAFTED DETAIL

*A crafted frame…
that looks simple
and somewhat
unpretentious.*

**THIS COTTAGE IS A BIT OF A MINI-ME.** Herb and Anne Rose had commissioned architects Lisa Botticelli and Ray Pohl to design a new vacation house on the north side of Nantucket. It was fairly large and contained a white, painted, partially open-framed central living area. They loved the look of that space so much that years later, when they acquired a partly renovated diminutive dwelling on the other side of the island a block and a half from the ocean, they asked Lisa and Ray to apply that same look to the whole cottage. They discarded the previous owners' unfinished renovations and started fresh with the original gabled forms, making modest cedar-clad additions in the spirit of the cottage's one-story human-scaled simple massing.

 The oversized entry door makes a statement centered between two quiet gray gables. The clear-finished mahogany screen door pops and also aligns with the opposite door out to the deck. "When they're both open, you really have that feeling of inside and outside being one," says Herb.

The modest, human-scaled gabled forms, clad entirely in weathered cedar and set on a generous wrapping deck, hug the landscape amid a frothy wake of *Rosa rugosa*.

**Architect:** Botticelli & Pohl
**Architects:** Lisa Botticelli
and Ray Pohl

Nantucket, Mass.

1,368 sq. ft.

N

Designed to appear as if it were an open porch that had been added and then enclosed, the sunroom is clad in weathered red-cedar boards that run horizontally at the base to suggest a guardrail, vertically to recall porch posts in between windows, and vertically to imply gable-end infill atop windows. A mahogany deck surrounds three sides of the cottage, seemingly doubling the living space.

The architects pulled forward what had been a deeply recessed entry between two matching gables to create more of an entry hall. And they reconfigured space to the north behind the original living-area fireplace to accommodate two new bathrooms. One serves the original west-facing bedroom, and the other, which includes a new bay for a claw-foot tub, serves a new east-facing master bedroom. A new sizable deck wraps three sides of the cottage and softly transitions to engage the site with robust *Rosa rugosa* foundation plantings and ornamental grasses. To the south, in the direction of the beach, they added a sunroom meant to look like a porch that had been added and later enclosed.

Upon first seeing the open framing throughout this cottage, I assumed it was strictly for summer use. The occasional wall closed in with beadboard had me further convinced because it seemed to reflect the often ad hoc treatment of older summer cottages. When I mentioned this to Herb he chuckled and said that Lisa would be so pleased that I had been duped. In fact, Lisa and Ray deliberately crafted the

  Centered below exposed sheltering rafters, the open living space enjoys both volume for gathering and intimacy for fireplace communing. Horizontal wide boards serve as an updated accent enclosing the fireplace chimney.

    The kitchen, also beneath a sheltering roof, includes a classic farmer's sink and soapstone counters. Floors throughout the cottage are fir. Informal overhead cabinets are open fronted. "It's easy to get to, not a lot of fuss. That's part of the whole aesthetic of the building," notes Lisa.

The open living/dining space extends through French doors into the uninsulated, bright sunroom. Anne's blue bottle collection positioned against the white framing and sheathing relates to classic blue and white seaside cottage furnishings.

The extra-wide entry door beneath the human-scaled lower ceiling opens into a hall finished with horizontal wide boards that offer a more contemporary accent and recall the board sheathing seen in the adjacent open living/dining area. Laundry machines are discreetly tucked into the closet behind the entry door.

The sunroom amps up the informal summer cottage sensibility via painted floors and center windows that open inward, thanks to an old-fashioned rope and pulley system (inspired by a similar configuration at an island restaurant that's no longer in business).

cottage frame for just such an appearance despite "outsulating" it with rigid foam on both the exterior walls and roof, and supplying it with central heat and air-conditioning. Herb notes, however, "It's costly to do it this way, though it looks simple and somewhat unpretentious." Because access to the site can be tricky in the winter, Herb and Anne don't generally use the cottage then, but they're always happy to have heat at the end of the spring and beginning of the fall seasons. They say they rarely use the air-conditioning.

The open plan of the living/dining area beneath the white, painted, open-framed sheltering roof sets an informal beachy tone. Having the kitchen open to the dining end of the living space, which continues on into the bright and airy sunroom extension helps the cottage live larger and comfortably for today. The generous wrapping deck expands living space out into the landscape for contemporary indoor–outdoor living. The new two-sided fireplace that serves the deck as well as the first-floor master bedroom increases the use of the deck on cooler evenings a few times a year when it's lit. "When you go on vacation, you want a simple sort of

 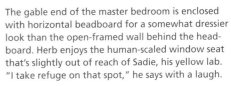

The gable end of the master bedroom is enclosed with horizontal beadboard for a somewhat dressier look than the open-framed wall behind the headboard. Herb enjoys the human-scaled window seat that's slightly out of reach of Sadie, his yellow lab. "I take refuge on that spot," he says with a laugh.

Lisa notes that the bathroom bay beneath the nestling sheltering roof was built around the claw-foot tub. Because the cottage is outsulated, the plumbing in front of the open framing is not at risk in the winter.

life—not necessarily one of deprivation or lacking in essential creature comforts but one that's easy, and not formal or demanding, and that doesn't require constant maintenance, so you can simply go relax and enjoy the elements," says Herb.

Lisa agrees. She and Ray strived to capture the simplicity Herb and Anne were looking for. "To me, this is a timeless piece of architecture because it's a pure definition of what I think a cottage would be," she says. Indeed, it's a cottage that reaches across time to both reflect a classic cottage of yore and embody a cottage for today.

# A MOTHER'S MODERN HAVEN

| ENGAGED WITH SITE | HUMAN SCALE | SIMPLE MASSING | SHELTERING ROOF | ECONOMY OF MEANS | INFORMALITY | SUNNY DISPOSITION | OPPOSITE COMPLEMENTS | WABI SABI | CRAFTED DETAIL |

**ARCHITECTS ARE PROBLEM SOLVERS,** and one problem that many architects relish is how to create something new and fresh in relation to something old or historic. Project Architect JT Loomis of Elliott + Elliott Architecture hit on a very clear idea early on when creating a concept board for a new winterized cottage for a family matriarch on their compound on Great Cranberry Island in Maine. He included a photo of quintessential Maine vernacular architecture: a white clapboard house with a detached simple, cedar-shingled barn. It was the historic pattern of a more formal main house in relation to a subordinate, unadorned work building that inspired the spare outbuilding aesthetic of the new cottage he designed to share property with the main original white clapboard farmhouse, owned by the family since the 1970s.

> The cottage reflects . . . the inside to the outside, the outside to the inside.

  Approached from the south, the mother's cottage sits on the west side of the property along a stand of spruce trees. Cedar clad and spare, it suggests an outbuilding to the original white farmhouse in the foreground and to the east. Its location and disposition engage the site to create an outdoor room between it and the farmhouse.

   The large openings in the gabled cottage further reduce its scale. Ipe slats on The Box's screen porch provide privacy and suggest, along with the steel supports and open steel stairs, a porous lightness that complements the more solid, simple massing of the cottage.

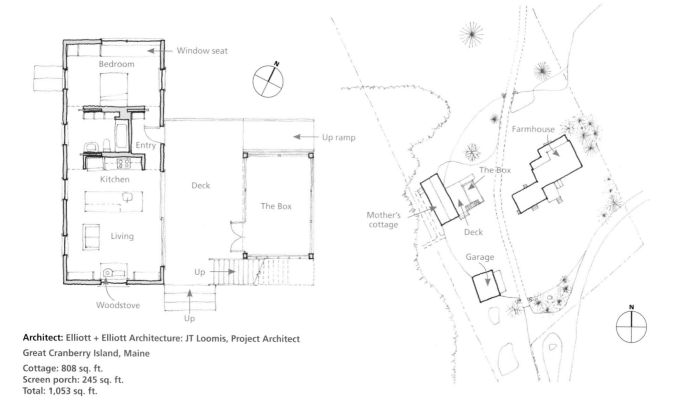

Window seat

Bedroom

N

Up ramp

Entry

Deck

The Box

Kitchen

Living

Up

Woodstove

Up

Farmhouse

The Box

Mother's
cottage

Deck

Garage

N

**Architect: Elliott + Elliott Architecture: JT Loomis, Project Architect**

**Great Cranberry Island, Maine**

Cottage: 808 sq. ft.
Screen porch: 245 sq. ft.
Total: 1,053 sq. ft.

    Oversized, custom, lift-slide mahogany doors with a 17-ft.-wide overall opening and the entry door farther down are connected and flanked by clear-finished, crafted mahogany slats. The total width of the mahogany assembly suggests one very wide opening. It plays with scale and relates overall to the width of the deck.

The ipe deck between the cottage and the screen Box, which features ipe slats on its southern face designed like the mahogany slats on the eastern face of the cottage, provides an informal, weathered-gray spillover space for outdoor living. "It's this wonderful playground/gathering space/private space when it needs to be. It has a lot of different uses," notes JT.

JT's initial charge had been to consider how to adapt an old failing second dwelling on the property for the matriarch to use. It was in approximately the same location of what would become the new cottage and had belonged previously to Margie Phippen, who was born in the early twentieth century and was the daughter of the Bulgers, who had owned the main house. Although Margie's former dwelling proved not to be salvageable, the current owners often refer to the new cottage that replaced it as the "Phippen House" after Margie and her husband, and they occasionally refer to the main house as the "Bulger House," as it's known on the island.

The new Phippen house is just large enough to accommodate the mother. "One of my purposes in moving over there was to get out of my married children's hair," she says. The married children include her daughter—who participated in and helped manage the design process—and her son, both of whom bring their young families with them to summer in the Bulger farmhouse. The new cottage is sited nudging the western property line to maximize space between it and the farmhouse on the east side of the property and to preserve the field in front of the farmhouse toward the northern water view. "We like that JT used the Maine barn style of vernacular; so even though it wasn't a traditional coastal house, it was congruent with the setting," says the daughter. The cottage includes an attached deck to the east, and a screen porch—complete with a roof deck offering stunning views toward the mountains of Acadia—sits to the east of the deck. The location and orientation of the new structures engage the site; together with the farmhouse, the structures define an outdoor grassy room, which is crossed by an informal unmarked foot path for neighbors en route to the beach.

 The screen porch dining space situated between the cottage and the farmhouse is a natural place for both households to meet to enjoy an informal meal together. When not in use, it also provides privacy between the cottage and the farmhouse. A steel stair with a stainless-steel cable rail that climbs on the south side of The Box is balanced by a ramp with a matching cable rail that descends on the north side.

The cottage's taut, elongated gabled form, clad almost entirely in shingles with minimal trim, reflects JT's modern interpretation of the quintessential spare outbuilding. It also reflects the simplicity and economy of means found in a new cottage. The human scale of the one-story dwelling and the simple massing of both it and the detached screen porch lend it cottage character. The cedar exterior and ipe decking, left to weather gray, evoke wabi sabi allure, and both the exterior finishes and the outdoor living embraced by the decks and screen porch suggest an informal barefoot cottage sensibility.

The screen porch structure has come to be called "The Box," largely because of its flat roof, which is a function of having a roof deck above. The Box was initially a bit controversial because it was seen as the most modern element. "We

believe that a design has different components to it, and one of those components is the time in which you live," notes JT. And the time in which we live embraces outdoor living. The screen porch offers a dining/gathering space for members of both the cottage and farmhouse households and a perch above to enjoy a cocktail while taking in the view. The Box also provides a privacy screen between the cottage and the farmhouse. "It serves us so well in so many ways," the mother remarks.

The cottage includes an open kitchen/living space with island-top dining for three, a full bathroom that borrows space from a hall that can be closed off by pocket doors on both ends, and a generous bedroom that can be closed off with pocket doors as well. The entry is part of the cottage's

   The open living area features a RAIS woodstove focal point in front of square windows that climb from floor to ceiling on the south wall beneath the sheltering ceiling. White shiplap walls and ceilings with a nickel gap between horizontal boards add a clean-line cottage touch.

  The core service space, which includes the kitchen's recessed cabinetry, is differentiated from the cathedral ceiling living spaces on either end of the cottage by both its quietly contrasting gray cabinetry color and the white plaster wall above, which interrupts what is meant to be read as the longer overall space finished with white horizontal shiplap. Oversized sliders wash the space with daylight.

The back hall runs past the bathroom, to which it contributes space, en route to the bedroom. Wide, barn-like, heart-pine floors add warmth and texture. Marvin tilt-turn windows receive minimal trim within the continuous shiplap walls so as not to distract.

The entry hall, which also sports heart-pine floors, abuts the bedroom, featuring gable-end large windows. A playful, narrow, Pivot Desk from Hive cleverly provides storage while occupying minimal depth.

core, which includes the bathroom and kitchen work area. The core's low ceiling provides more intimate and task-oriented compressed space, which is complemented by the tall cathedral ceiling of the open kitchen/living area and bedroom. Three large square windows climb toward the ceiling of the sheltering gable living area to welcome southern daylight in addition to the eastern light that washes in through the oversized sliders off the more public space. White shiplap with ⅛-in. nickel gaps between boards expresses a consistent economy of means, finishing the interior cathedral ceilings and walls of the open public space and the bedroom.

The family is as happy with the interior of the cottage as they are with how the exterior relates to the property. "It has integrity. It reflects entirely what it is—the inside to the outside, the outside to the inside," says the mother. Her daughter notes, "Inside, it's very calming. It's very harmonious. It makes the most of a small amount of space." They're particularly happy with how the cottage accommodates their extended family. "The things I would spend more time doing in real life I can do in my cottage because it's an escape. It's a different scene. In this case, it's an opportunity to be with my family and do things together," says the mother.

 The bedroom beneath the sheltering ceiling is cloaked in white shiplap, which contributes scale and texture. The window seat, built into the millwork storage wall, is a favorite destination for the grandkids. Ample daylight animates the space.

# RENEWED AND IMPROVED

ENGAGED WITH SITE · HUMAN SCALE · SIMPLE MASSING · SHELTERING ROOF · ECONOMY OF MEANS · INFORMALITY · SUNNY DISPOSITION · OPPOSITE COMPLEMENTS · WABI SABI · CRAFTED DETAIL

**IT'S NOT EVERY DAY THAT A HOMEOWNER APPROACHES** an architect whom they're considering retaining to design a renovation/addition and says, "We love our house." Usually a homeowner leads with the aspect of their house that is wanting. But for Piper and Chris Underwood, they had fallen in love with their 1950s-era house in Del Mar, Calif., 10 years earlier. "It touched me in its simplicity and modesty," says Piper, who was particularly enamored with the private rear yard punctuated at the end by a huge pine tree. But, in the intervening years, their two boys were becoming teenagers and the narrow shared living areas and dubious wiring and plumbing were in need of improvement. The challenge for architect Nick Noyes would be to address the shortcomings without compromising the existing cottage's character. Piper and Chris wanted more breathing room, but they didn't want to expand into the rear yard they loved.

*Informal… but impressive enough when it needs to be.*

A humble fence, painted the same rusty red as the board-and-batten cottage, defines a front courtyard composed of economical, concrete stepping-stones and gravel strips.

Straight ahead, the butter-colored paneled porch wall, beneath the sheltering Galvalume roof, is differentiated enough from the board-and-batten to announce the entry.

The new guest room has its own entrance (flanked by cottagey bee blossom) off the front courtyard, which provides both additional privacy and informal outdoor living space. Even though this western wing was widened and had its ridge raised, it still expresses human scale within simple massing.

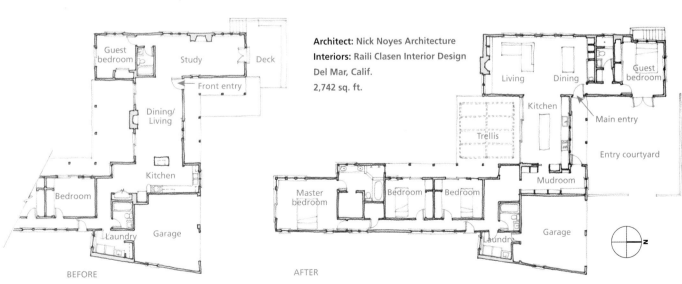

**Architect:** Nick Noyes Architecture
**Interiors:** Raili Clasen Interior Design
Del Mar, Calif.
**2,742 sq. ft.**

BEFORE

- Guest bedroom
- Study
- Deck
- Front entry
- Dining/ Living
- Kitchen
- Bedroom
- Laundry
- Garage

AFTER

- Living
- Dining
- Guest bedroom
- Kitchen
- Trellis
- Main entry
- Entry courtyard
- Master bedroom
- Bedroom
- Bedroom
- Mudroom
- Laundry
- Garage

 The dining area, right off the new entrance, sits beneath the sheltering roof's painted, exposed framing and rod ties. A new bar features accent black cabinets and a black-and-white photo mural of an old truck from Chris's family wine and spirits distribution business, which dates back to 1875. A simple, white, painted-board barn slider closes off the bar when not in use.

Nick observed that the cottage should better connect with the rear and front yards—to the south and north, respectively—to maximize outdoor living while maintaining privacy. He also aimed to improve flow between the primary living spaces of the kitchen, dining, and living areas so the cottage would work better on a daily basis for the family of four as well as when the family entertains larger groups. He and the owners agreed that the bedroom wing, which they believed to be a somewhat newer addition, would need little changed other than some new finishes.

Because the original cottage's simple massing and human scale were among its charms, Nick was careful to discreetly incorporate more floor area and volume. He widened the western wing that runs north–south just enough to absorb the width of a former entry porch and lengthened it in the direction of a former deck to the north, while also raising the ridge a modest 18 in. or so. The result added approximately 300 sq. ft. and subtly increased the volume of that wing, all while maintaining the simple massing and human scale. The new, exposed sheltering roof framing and painted-steel tie rods add rhythm and texture. New eaves mimic the existing overhanging crafted rafter-tail details, and new siding mimics the original redwood no-nonsense board-and-batten finish. The increased width and length of that wing in combination with the taller cathedral ceiling there now accommodates a relocated dining/living area to the south (anchored by a new fireplace) and a new guest room and full bath to the north. (Before the renovation, the south end of that wing contained a smaller guest room and full bath, which blocked daylight and view of the more private rear yard from the living area.)

Memories of a raised concrete hearth in Piper's childhood home inspired the design of a similar hearth in the living area, which relates to the new board-formed concrete Rumford fireplace there. The main entry now opens directly into the new dining/living area approached from a shallow porch off the new protected entry court.

Because the kitchen is often the center of attention at a gathering, and even when not entertaining, it was moved into the center of the house to be part of the action. Previously, it had been tucked in a small ell against the garage wall to the east. It now occupies the space between the new front entry court—seen through new kitchen windows to the north—and the reimagined back patio to the south, accessed via oversized sliders in a wall that had once been partially interrupted by a daylight- and view-blocking fireplace. The large and informal galley kitchen is open to the dining/living area, but its relationship, perpendicular to it through a cased opening, offers it some separation as well. The new location floods the cooking area with daylight and connects it to outdoor living in front and back, which allows this small house to live a little larger. A mudroom and pantry now take the place of the former kitchen.

*(continued on p. 55)*

 The living area, beyond the open dining area, includes a new utilitarian yet sophisticated board-formed, concrete Rumford fireplace and plenty of space for the family, which makes it one of Piper's favorite places in the cottage.

The raised hearth of the reading nook not only provides cozy additional seating but also positions the fireplace at eye level when family and guests are seated. The window seat, partially beneath an intimate soffit, complements the volume of the cathedral ceiling in the living space it borders.

   Nick opened the kitchen wing to the front entry courtyard via a run of square Marvin windows above the counter to the north and to the rear yard via oversized Weiland glass sliders to the south. This allows the interior to borrow space and daylight from the outdoors and for the interior to expand outdoors.

   The efficient galley kitchen includes rift-sawn, white-oak custom cabinets with a stain that blends well with the engineered white-oak flooring, which warms the mostly white palette running through the kitchen and dining/living wings. The view from the kitchen sink wall extends across the front porch and into the entry court, which acts as a buffer to the street.

Because the kitchen wing is perpendicular to the dining/living wing, which is accessed through a large cased opening, it's both part of the dining/living area and somewhat distinct from it. The cohesive palette helps unify the perpendicular spaces. The kitchen also benefits from a sheltering roof and brass hardware, which will acquire an appealing patina.

The new pantry/mudroom occupies the former kitchen. The floor is the original durable concrete with a new thinset finish, and the ceiling is flat and lower to suit the utilitarian space. The black mudroom bench and tall pantry storage cabinetry along with the black peg rail and black-and-white checkerboard wallpaper introduce playful black accents, which also appear in the bar area and elsewhere.

*(continued from p. 51)*

Interior designer Raili Clasen joined the team to help with interior finishes and furnishings. Nick established the consistent and economic backdrop of mostly white interior walls, ceilings, and trim, and worked with Raili and the owners to create some feature moments. They all agreed that oak accents in the form of the engineered prefinished oak flooring in the kitchen and living/dining areas and rift-sawn, white-oak cabinetry with a stain in the kitchen and the desk built-in (behind barn sliders off the new guest room) would warm those spaces and also help unify them. They opted for brass fixtures in the kitchen and brass hardware on the doors and kitchen cabinets to similarly add warmth while introducing a pleasing wabi sabi patina and substantial feel. Raili proposed the black cabinetry accents in the bar behind the barn sliders off the dining area and in the pantry/mudroom as well as the black-and-white wallpaper in those locations, which act as bookends of sorts to the kitchen. Black details in the rugs, pillows, and guest room linens weave the sophisticated yet playful look into the soft finishes, too.

After the project was complete, Nick was pleased to hear Piper report that Chris said that he could stay there forever. Although much of the cottage is essentially new now, it's still familiar enough to evoke the essence of the cottage that originally attracted Piper. "Our house doesn't feel large when it's just the four of us; it still feels cozy; but when we have larger groups, everyone has a place to sit," says Piper. "It's a very informal house, but it's impressive enough when it needs to be," notes Nick of the cottage he shaped for how the Underwoods live today.

Just outside the kitchen sliders, a willow-covered, lightweight, galvanized steel arbor designed by Nick provides informal, shaded shelter for outdoor seating, overlooking the backyard and large pine that won Piper's heart from the outset.

# OVER WATER LIVING

| ENGAGED WITH SITE | HUMAN SCALE | SIMPLE MASSING | SHELTERING ROOF | ECONOMY OF MEANS | INFORMALITY | SUNNY DISPOSITION | OPPOSITE COMPLEMENTS | WABI SABI | CRAFTED DETAIL |

A unique connection to its waterfront site.

**KEN AND DEE GRAY LOVED THE LOCATION** of the house on Newbury Neck, which had once been a concession stand for the Blue Hill Fair in Maine and was sited primarily over the water with a terrace below, but they didn't love the crumbling rubble basement foundation or the cramped rooms. Though they first considered trying to rehab it and replacing the foundation with new piers, they decided in consultation with Elliott + Elliott Architecture that such action would not only be cost prohibitive but also, to put it mildly, a logistical challenge on the merely 6,098-sq.-ft. lot. After meeting with the town regulators and the Maine Department of Environmental Protection, the owners and their architects learned that a new house could be constructed on the property no closer to the water than the house they planned to replace and could expand by up to 30 percent of the volume or floor area, whichever was most limiting.

The simple massing of the sheltering shed-roofed open living/dining/kitchen waterfront component and flanking flat-roofed service and bedroom street-front component expresses clarity of function and hierarchy. Perched atop piers, the composition might also be said to resemble a collection of casual fishing cottages.

   Supported by piers, some of which land on the granite terrace below, the lightly weathered white cedar–clad cottage extends over the bay.

From the street, the one-story flat-roofed volume relates to the scale of the neighboring houses. The clerestory windows above draw southwestern light into the shed-roofed volume that faces the bay. The recessed entry is accessed from a bridge edged with unassuming nautical-inspired cable rails.

The front wall of the cottage is pulled back from the front granite retaining wall to create greater distance between the house and the street. The gap between is bridged at the entry and again here to access the deck. Corey notes that at high tide, light reflects off the bay onto the underside of the house and bounces back onto the sloped riprap.

**Architect: Elliott + Elliott Architecture: Corey Papadopoli, Project Architect**

Surry, Maine

1,478 sq. ft.

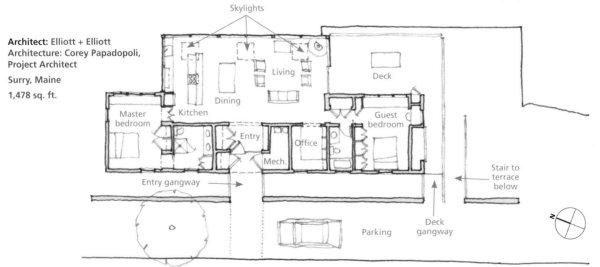

Skylights

Living

Deck

Dining

Master bedroom

Kitchen

Guest bedroom

Entry

Office

Mech.

Stair to terrace below

Entry gangway

Parking

Deck gangway

N

Because volume proved to be more limiting, the architects did a series of three-dimensional studies exploring different massing solutions that might maximize the allowable volume. Ken and Dee were looking for a two-bedroom, two-bathroom dwelling with an open concept living/dining/kitchen area and water access from a terrace below. "Being small was good from my point of view," says Ken. They also hoped to push it farther than 4 ft. from the road, which was how close the original house had been.

The architects' solution was to anchor the bank with a granite retaining wall along a cobbled parking area, stabilize the slope with fieldstone riprap, and construct the house on a series of 14-in.-dia. reinforced-concrete-filled fiberglass piers. They pulled the front wall of the cottage back from the retaining wall at the top of the bank in order to gain greater distance between it and the road. As a result, you enter the cottage across a short ipe bridge that is thick enough to house all of the utilities entering the building as well. Another narrower bridge provides side access to the ipe deck on the eastern, water side of the cottage. A granite stair directly off the parking area leads down to a lower granite terrace that sits on a foundation mat. There, a granite stair that's the full width of the terrace descends directly into the water, literally engaging the site.

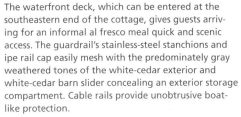

The waterfront deck, which can be entered at the southeastern end of the cottage, gives guests arriving for an informal al fresco meal quick and scenic access. The guardrail's stainless-steel stanchions and ipe rail cap easily mesh with the predominately gray weathered tones of the white-cedar exterior and white-cedar barn slider concealing an exterior storage compartment. Cable rails provide unobtrusive boat-like protection.

The freshwater pearl granite terrace steps down between the 12-ft.-on-center piers to directly access the water below the cottage. The fiberglass exteriors of the piers are painted a custom color inspired by Ellsworth schist to blend in with the neutral palette. Ken stores his ocean-rowing shell on a pulley system below the cottage.

A strip of clear glass in the entry door and side lite at eye level allow Ken and Dee to see who's arriving, while frosted glass saves the bulk of the view through to the water until those entering are indoors. The lower ceiling at the entry provides a compressed transition from the outdoors to the spatial release of the cathedral ceiling.

The living area beneath the sheltering ceiling enjoys a stellar view through floor-to-ceiling windows and oversized glass sliders out to the deck. Afternoon light also streams in from the clerestory windows and skylights. The low teak cabinet in front of the window, custom made so as to not interrupt the view, contains a 36-in. TV attached to the lid which flips up for viewing.

Opting for flat roofs above human-scaled, one-story bedroom and service spaces along the street meant the architects could include more volume beneath a sheltering shed roof above shared living/dining/kitchen space toward the water. The resulting simple massing is both legible and practical. Project Architect Corey Papadopoli notes, "I'm a big believer in programmatic transparency, so what happens inside is reflected outside." The architects elected for the shed roof to slope up away from the bay to capture additional southwestern light through operable clerestory windows above the adjacent flat roof. And they incorporated fixed floor-to-ceiling glass toward the water view in the northeast wall below the lower end of the shed slope. Operable skylights near the floor-to-ceiling window wall offer bonus daylighting and ventilation, in addition to that provided by the oversized sliders out to the deck.

A limited palette of minimally trimmed white cedar shingles on the exterior walls of the flat-roof subordinate spaces and vertical white cedar on the exterior walls of the shed-roof volume subtly differentiates the two, while communicating an economy of means. With time, both volumes will further weather a soft gray, gently blending in with the shoreline, as will the ipe decking. A similarly spare and cohesive palette inside, which includes unobtrusive, flush, crafted trim, likewise minimizes distraction, allowing the focus to be on the view

Ken and Dee chose calming Benjamin Moore Gray Cashmere paint for the walls throughout the cottage. The kitchen island discreetly maximizes storage and is painted one tone darker, Benjamin Moore Misted Green. Glass shelves for glassware are quietly suspended from a steel plate hidden within the top shelf in front of an operable kitchen window.

outside, effectively bringing the outdoors in and the indoors out. Simple, flat, lower plaster ceilings over the bedroom and service areas provide for more intimate and task-oriented spaces, complementing the soaring yet sheltering ceiling of painted Glulam rafters and structural decking over the open, informal living/dining/kitchen common areas.

Ken and Dee have found that their contemporary coastal cottage is very easy to take care of and that its simplicity also makes it easy for both them and others to use and enjoy. Its unique connection to its waterfront site allows them to commune with the natural world of the bay, from both within the cottage and out on the deck and terrace where Ken launches his ocean rowing shell.

They've seen seals, a dolphin, and all sorts of water fowl, including a great blue heron, which visited almost daily for a while on its hunting rounds. Dee notes that if you were to spend the day simply engaged with the view, you would never grow bored.

The master bedroom beneath a lower, more intimately scaled ceiling features focused framed views and daylight through operable triple-glazed Drewexim windows (no longer distributed in the United States). As was done elsewhere in the cottage, narrow window trim is mounted flush with a reveal so as not to distract or obtrude.

# LOYALIST TODAY

ENGAGED WITH SITE

HUMAN SCALE

SIMPLE MASSING

SHELTERING ROOF

ECONOMY OF MEANS

INFORMALITY

SUNNY DISPOSITION

WABI SABI

CRAFTED DETAIL

Intimate yet unconfined spaces.

**FOR YEARS, LOIS AND KEN LIPPMANN** had been walking by and admiring the Loyalist Cottage when visiting Harbour Island in the Bahamas. Originally built in 1797, it's the oldest of the Loyalist cottages on island. Lois and Ken, who hail from North Salem, N.Y., love antique houses and found the simple massing of the porch-fronted, petite Loyalist Cottage irresistible. They also appreciated that the family who had long owned it included a celebrated bonefish fisherman. Ken is a bonefish fisherman too. When they heard the cottage owners might consider selling, Ken and Lois made an offer. They

The view (now reconstructed) of the diminutive charmer along the water is what pulled at Lois and Ken's heartstrings. The simple massing of the side-facing gable and front sheltering porch is classic cottage. The doghouse-style dormers—complete with six-lite over six-lite double-hung windows peering out of the roof—seem to blink "hello."

The porch's sheltering roof with exposed rafters and unadorned trimmed posts, all painted the same white as the exterior Dutch-lap siding, is informal and cheerful. The porch is just deep enough to comfortably accommodate a line of colorful reclined porch chairs, perfect for gazing at the sea.

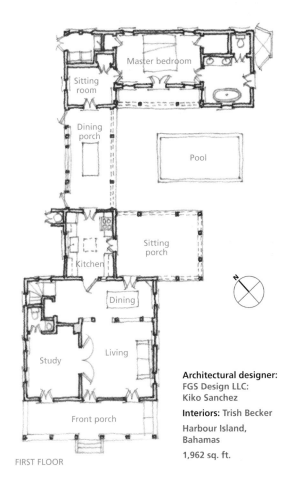

FIRST FLOOR

**Architectural designer:**
FGS Design LLC:
Kiko Sanchez

**Interiors:** Trish Becker

Harbour Island,
Bahamas

1,962 sq. ft.

hadn't even seen the inside. Once they did, they discovered it needed quite a bit of work. But their offer had been accepted. So off they went to mull it over at Sip Sip, a local eatery in town, where they got a tip that led them to meet and engage their project team: architectural designer Kiko Sanchez, who worked with a local architect of record, and designer Trish Becker.

Lois and Ken wanted to add a new master bedroom suite to augment the two second-floor bedrooms in the original cottage. But first they needed to replace the failing original foundation. When contractors lifted the cottage to do so, the cottage began to crack and buckle. The Lippmanns ended up with little choice but to tear it down and rebuild it stick by stick, salvaging as much original material as possible. But as with many unfortunate turn of events, there was also hidden opportunity. Kiko suggested that they build the interior back as a mirror image of the original layout. He flipped the plan, so the support spaces of the stairs, powder room, and study edge what had become a busy side road, and the living and dining areas face the sunnier side yard to the southeast. This also enabled direct connection to the sitting porch off the dining area and view beyond to where they installed a new pool within a new outdoor room defined by ell-shaped additions off the rear kitchen.

 The original sitting porch includes a new custom-crafted guardrail above and louvered shutters that admit breezes while providing privacy from neighbors. The floor is coralina stone, much like the original, which expresses age with wabi sabi appeal.

They salvaged enough of the original, wide Dutch-lap siding to face the front of the cottage, and they clad much of the rest with the slightly narrower Dutch lap that's currently available. The paneled window and door shutters match the original, but Lois modified the color a bit to make it a slightly deeper, yet still sunny, aqua. "It's the color of the sea," she says. The local hardware store now carries the color and calls it "Loyalist." The sitting porch is also original to the house, but Kiko dressed up the flat roof with a custom-crafted guardrail that he modeled on another well-known house in the Bahamas, the Jacaranda House in Nassau.

Kiko's design challenge was to incorporate a new rear building to house a human-scaled, one-story master suite, so it relates to the main building and positively engages the site. He did so by connecting it to a new dining porch that abuts the rear kitchen, such that both new spaces and the existing sitting porch all overlook the pool. Lois says that the new dining porch can accommodate an informal dinner party of 10. "There's an axis that runs through the front door, across the kitchen, across the dining porch, and all the way to the sitting room," notes Kiko. This allows Ken to see straight out to their dock and the sea from his study/sitting room when the front door is open.

Inside the original cottage on the main level, exposed floor joists overhead, a dropped carrying beam received by posts on a half wall, and vertical-board finished walls—all painted a semi-gloss linen white color—create intimate, yet unconfined spaces. Upstairs, the board finish on the walls is rotated horizontally to echo the horizontal-board finish on the sheltering ceiling rafters. The consistent palette, which

*(continued on p. 68)*

 A custom built-in bench with louvered shutters behind provides an informal, comfortable landing spot on the sitting porch off both the kitchen and indoor dining areas. The muted pillows and cushions softly pick up on the calm palette of the beige coralina stone and aqua shutters and pool.

 There's even a mini porch on the front of the master suite. That makes for three porches, shaping three sides of an outdoor pool room. A fence (not shown) defines the fourth edge. The same exterior palette from the original cottage extends to the master suite.

The new informal dining porch connector is centered below the intimately scaled exposed structure of a sheltering roof. Louvered shutters welcome air, cut western glare, and provide privacy—here, from the side street. The narrow French doors of the study align with the front entrance French doors and the new dock out front; you can see the water reflected in the glass of the study doors.

The semi-open first floor of the original cottage includes the re-created crafted posts and half wall that differentiate the front living area and the dining area. The rhythm of the joists overhead, the textured board walls, and divided-lite French doors and double-hung windows lend interest, scale, and detail while adhering to the mostly linen-white color palette.

The renovated galley kitchen beneath a sheltering roof and ceiling features encaustic cement tiles, known as Cuban tiles, which pick up on the calming linen-white color palette. A farmer's sink and open shelves with crafted brackets add an informal touch. The dining porch is a convenient step or two away.

*(continued from p. 64)*

includes contrasting dark, stained, mahogany floors (except for in the kitchen and bathrooms), allows the spaces to blend together. The new master suite picks up on the same material and color palette, only used more sparingly. The wall finish there is plaster, but the sheltering tray ceilings of the bedroom and bathroom receive the same board treatment as the ceilings in the original cottage.

The renovated and new spaces include modern amenities without calling attention to them. Most notably, the new, somewhat more generous spaces flow effortlessly from the original cottage and create expansive informal outdoor living, which better suits a cottage for today. "In that climate, you want to be outdoors," says Lois.

 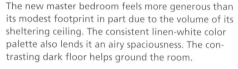 The new master bedroom feels more generous than its modest footprint in part due to the volume of its sheltering ceiling. The consistent linen-white color palette also lends it an airy spaciousness. The contrasting dark floor helps ground the room.

 Upstairs, in the original cottage, a guest bedroom tucks underneath the sheltering roof. A cozy window seat takes advantage of the headroom the dormer provides. The horizontal, linen-white board-finish walls and ceiling help unify and seemingly enlarge the bright space.

# TWIN GABLES

ENGAGED WITH SITE    HUMAN SCALE    SIMPLE MASSING    SHELTERING ROOF    ECONOMY OF MEANS    INFORMALITY    SUNNY DISPOSITION    OPPOSITE COMPLEMENTS    WABI SABI    CRAFTED DETAIL

**IT HELPS TO HAVE A SPECTACULAR SITE** with a view direction and street orientation that are in sync with daylighting and backyard privacy. The front street side of Molly and Bill Donovan's property faces northwest, and the back overlooks a broad view of tidal marshes, the mouth of the Spurwink River, and Higgins Beach beyond to the southeast. It's in a much less crowded neighborhood than where Molly and Bill used to have a cottage in nearby, densely packed Higgins Beach. Still there are neighbors on both sides.

> The design nods to the cottages of the Higgins Beach community.

Maximizing the buildable footprint within the simple massing of peaked gables interrupted by a glass-enclosed stairwell, the front of the cottage greets those arriving with a modest porch. Eastern white-cedar shingles with a bleaching-oil finish and steeply pitched gables offer cottage curb appeal.

 The water side of the cottage boasts a large radial wall of glass, brimmed with a shed roof that not only provides shade from harsh sunlight when the sun is high in the sky but also helps bring the overall scale of the cottage down. Barely visible in this shot, solar panels above the guest room shed dormer and gable (to the left) provide most of the electrical power required by the house.

**Architect:** Winkelman
**Architecture:** Will Winkelman
**Scarborough, Maine**
**1,980 sq. ft.**

FIRST FLOOR

Lower deck

Upper deck

Living

Dining

Kitchen

Open to above

Garage

Laundry

Den

Entry

Mudroom

Front porch

SECOND FLOOR

Master bedroom

South deck

Bridge

Open to below

Guest bedroom

Loft above

North deck

N

 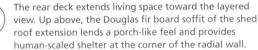

The rear deck extends living space toward the layered view. Up above, the Douglas fir board soffit of the shed roof extension lends a porch-like feel and provides human-scaled shelter at the corner of the radial wall.

Just inside the low-ceiling entry-way, light spilling from above into the stair hall straight ahead entices those arriving toward the view beyond the French doors. Bill notes that when those doors are open, "You could not feel like you're living more outside when you're inside."

When architect Will Winkelman laid out the year-round cottage, he lengthened it parallel to the view to maximize visual access and bolstered the east side with a more con-tained den and the west side with a one-car garage to secure privacy from the adjacent neighbors. Then to the southeast he introduced a dramatic, faceted wall of transom-topped glass doors and windows—like an amped up bay—to fully engage the stunning site. "I always feel as though to address a view, you want to be reasonably square to it," explains Will. Recognizing that you also want to be protected from direct, harsh daylight when the sun is high in the sky, he incorpo-rated a porch-like, sheltering shed-roof brim over the top of the transom windows. The brim is just deep enough to

  A gas fireplace picture-framed with a fresh-water, pearled-granite surround adds a contemporary cozy touch to the faceted wall of glass oriented toward the sweeping view. An oil painting on canvas of Maine lobster boats by Jill Hoy hangs over the fireplace.

provide late afternoon shade in the temperate seasons but not so deep as to block low daylight from entering in the winter.

One potential risk of a longer house is that the middle can be relatively dark. But an advantage is that spaces at either end can have greater privacy from each other. To address the potential risk and rewards of a longer footprint, Will introduced a prominent stair in the middle to act as a light well and to reinforce the second-floor privacy between a master suite on the east end and a guest suite on the west end. First visible from the entryway, which has a lower ceiling than the main living area, the stairwell draws those entering toward its taller volume and the light flooding down from above, as well as the view beyond it out the radial window wall. The soaring space of the open stairwell effectively complements the compressed entry space, which makes a memorable entry sequence for such a small cottage.

  The simple palette of Douglas fir board walls with Monocoat finish wraps the kitchen and stairs, visually tying them together. Engineered oak floors and oak guardrail elements, also with a Monocoat finish, similarly unify the multipurpose space.

The kitchen breakfast bar boasts a stellar view. Full overlay cabinetry, which is typically associated with a contemporary design, is teamed here with legs, a more traditional detail. The result is a transitional look that's reinforced by the cabinet doors' wide stiles and rails. The white of the cabinets and quartz countertops suit the palette of clean white ceilings and trim.

Second-floor decks on both the front and back off the stair hall are accessed by glass doors within considerable window runs. Together, the decks and glazing further strengthen the connection between indoors and out and provide daylight to the center of the cottage on both levels. "The design of the decks . . . gives us that flexibility to be where we wanted to be outdoors," notes Bill. "We follow the sun," adds Molly. The glassy stair hall is capped with a low-sloped gable roof that connects the taller twin gables of the bedrooms, resulting in legible, simple massing.

The first-floor semi-open plan cleverly tucks the main working portion of the kitchen around the corner toward the garage, out of sight of the living area. An informal breakfast bar counter extends along the faceted window wall toward the open dining area, which is flexible enough to comfortably accommodate a round table—for four when the Donovans are entertaining another couple—or the oval table it becomes, which seats eight to ten. The nearby den offers a more private space to tuck away and watch TV. In the future, if need be, it could serve as a first-floor master bedroom suite.

A board-wall treatment wraps much of the first floor and continues up the stairs to the second-floor stair hall, helping one flow into the other with an economy of means. Composed of Douglas fir with nickel-thickness gaps between the boards and a Rubio Monocoat finish that lends it a driftwood appearance, it warms the interior, adds texture, and contributes to a cottage feel. A white-oak guardrail system similarly treated with a muted Monocoat finish includes cable wires that offer an informal nautical touch that is echoed in the red-cedar and cable-wire guardrail on the decks. Radiant-heated floors topped with engineered white oak, also treated with a Monocoat finish, can be found throughout the cottage.

It was important to Molly and Bill that their small home's design nods to the cottages of the Higgins Beach community while reflecting more how the Donovans like to live now. Molly notes, "It does look pretty cottagey, but modern at the same time." Bill agrees.

During a site visit while the cottage was being constructed, the design team observed that there would be room for a small loft above the guest bedroom. Molly and Bill loved the idea. It's become a favorite play and nap spot for their grandkids.

 Though the master bedroom footprint is modest, the volume of the raised 12-ft. 6-in. ceiling lends it spaciousness. Double-hung windows, with two lites over two lites, are a nod to the cottage tradition of divided lites, but with a less busy pattern.

 The patina of the rough driftwood-like finish of the wide Douglas fir boards installed with a crisp nickel-thickness gap between them demonstrates how opposites can complement each other in a material treatment and its installation. The finely crafted guardrails on the stairs and decks share the same design to help further blur the line between inside and outside.

# HIDDEN IN PLAIN SIGHT

ENGAGED WITH SITE

HUMAN SCALE

SIMPLE MASSING

SHELTERING ROOF

ECONOMY OF MEANS

INFORMALITY

SUNNY DISPOSITION

OPPOSITE COMPLEMENTS

WABI SABI

CRAFTED DETAIL

**YOU NEVER KNOW WHAT YOU MIGHT DISCOVER** one afternoon if you set out on a short drive from your house with a little time on your hands and some curiosity. You might take that winding road through the woods that you've never explored before, and it just might open up to a lake that you never realized was there, ringed by property with terrific views. That's how one of the homeowners in this story came to discover the area in Canaan, N.H., that would become home to the vacation cottage she shares with her husband and their two teenage sons, just a 15-minute or so drive from their primary residence. "I'm finding that having this place so close to us is really convenient, because we use it a lot more than we would use a house if it were a couple of hours away," she says.

Everybody just spills out onto the porch or front lawn…

Off to one side of the property, the cottage with its simple massing and quiet exterior palette enjoys the expanse and terrain of the property and lakeside view, while fitting into it.

     Oriented with the gable ends to the lake and the street, the cottage greets those arriving from the driveway with a protected, hooded entrance beneath simple shed dormers in the sheltering roof. Shingles on the upper story and clapboards on the lower story break up the wall finish, so the cottage doesn't appear overly tall.

  The person-scaled, sheltering, gable hood at the entry is supported by brackets rather than posts, so it doesn't compete visually with the post-supported, water-side porch. The fir ceiling matches that on the porch. Can you see why the owners refer to the cottage as the "Bird's Nest"?

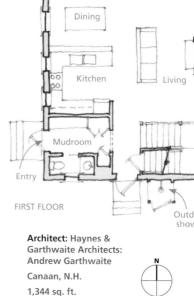

Screen porch

Dining

Kitchen

Living

Mudroom

Entry

FIRST FLOOR

Outdoor shower

**Architect:** Haynes & Garthwaite Architects: Andrew Garthwaite

Canaan, N.H.

1,344 sq. ft.

The screen porch, detailed as if it were an open porch infilled with screen panels, expands living into the landscape overlooking the lake. The steps off the side of the porch lead to the grill-with-a-view area.

Sited in the approximate location of an old trailer that had occupied the site previously, the family's new cottage, designed by Andrew Garthwaite of Haynes & Garthwaite Architects, sits on the north corner of the property, rather than in the center, where it overlooks the lake as well as the rest of the property. There are a number of large rock outcrops to which they chose to relate the cottage in order to best engage the site. The wife's preference was to orient the cottage's simple massing such that the gable end would be seen from the lake. Andrew had proposed some earlier schemes in which the long side of the cottage was parallel to the water, but the owners prefer the living spaces more unified and consolidated ending in the lake, rather than strung out along it.

Andrew designed the first floor with unusually tall (9-ft.) ceilings for a cottage of its size so as to accommodate extra-tall (8-ft.) doors toward the lake that both bring in lots of light and maximize view from the informal open living/dining/kitchen area. The wife knew that she wanted the second-floor bedrooms nestled beneath dormers within a sheltering roof, which also keeps the cottage from appearing overly tall. "I like the rooms on the inside with those dormers, with the light and the angles that you get in the ceiling of the rooms," she says. Andrew chose shed dormers instead of, for example, gable dormers because shed dormers are simpler, less fussy. The two bedrooms on the water side of the cottage have prime views of the lake and are nearly identical. A third, smaller bedroom in the back has an angled view to the water in the winter. All the bedrooms share a full bathroom. "The homeowners wanted it as flexible as possible," notes Andrew, and they didn't feel the privacy of a nested bathroom off a master bedroom was necessary. Plus, there's an outdoor shower at what they consider the back of the cottage, which speaks to the informality of the cottage's barefoot living.

Downstairs, you enter into a mudroom from the driveway side of the cottage opposite the stairs to the full unfinished

   The living/dining/kitchen area enjoys a 9-ft.-tall open space with 8-ft.-tall doors, creating an airy, daylight-filled room that embraces the lake beyond. The light, light-blue ceiling and sand-colored walls bring some outdoor colors inside.

 Six-ft.-tall windows in the living area, which align with the top of the 8-ft.-tall doors, are scaled up too, helping the space feel more generous, brighter, and better connected to the outdoors. Soapstone (like the nearby kitchen counters) surrounds the gas fireplace, and a reclaimed timber mantel adds texture as well as a dash of wabi sabi to the clean, fresh palette.

The efficient open kitchen is partially screened from the dining area with a cherry-capped half wall. A beadboard wainscot runs around the open space to protect the walls and reduce their apparent height. That's the faucet of a salvaged farmer's sink peaking above the half wall. You can stand at the sink and take in the view of the lake unobstructed.

The porch posts and warm porch ceiling frame the lake view from the dining table, bringing the lake experience inside and the dining experience outside. The chandelier is on a pulley system, so it can be raised above dining view or lowered for a game of cards, as need be.

basement and up to the bedrooms. The rest of the floor is open to the living/dining/kitchen area, which, in turn, opens onto the human-scaled porch. The color palette of the tall, open first floor picks up on the colors outside, with walls the color of beach sand and a ceiling the light, light blue color of the sky. On the narrower space of the porch, beneath the shed roof sloping down toward the lake, the ceiling is crafted, clear-finished fir, suggesting a warmer interior treatment, the opposite complement of the cool sky-inspired color on the tall ceiling inside. The interior color palette downstairs continues upstairs, helping unify the spaces of the small cottage.

"When you've got a lot of people there—it's usually good weather if you've got a lot of people there—everybody just spills out onto the porch or the front lawn, and it doesn't feel cramped in any way," says the husband. The connection to the landscape is part of what particularly suits their cottage to contemporary living. They also prefer the open plan,

The screen porch is wide enough to accommodate informal dining on one end and sitting on the other, both basking in sunshine and the lake view. The sheltering shed ceiling with warm fir finish adds cozy interior warmth to complement the cool blue outdoor expanse of sky and water beyond the screens.

something that's more common in cottages today. "It feels more inviting," the wife says. And it allows a view of the lake from all of the spaces. Another part of what makes the cottage timely is convenience, both in terms of its relative location and its uncomplicated use, including that it can mostly be heated by the gas fireplace because it's very well insulated. "It's really easy to live there. Very little maintenance," the husband notes. You just might want to go for a short drive in your neck of the woods to see if there's a plum piece of property ripe for a vacation cottage—to be newly constructed or renovated—hiding in plain sight.

Tucked beneath a wide shed dormer within the sheltering roof, the front corner bedroom enjoys daylight from two directions, cross ventilation, and a lovely treetop view of the lake below. The same fresh and airy interior palette as downstairs integrates this upstairs bedroom, like the others, with the rest of the cottage.

# FLOATING AND FOOTLOOSE

ENGAGED WITH SITE · HUMAN SCALE · SIMPLE MASSING · SHELTERING ROOF · ECONOMY OF MEANS · INFORMALITY · SUNNY DISPOSITION · OPPOSITE COMPLEMENTS · WABI SABI · CRAFTED DETAIL

Inspiration found in aging waterfront warehouses.

**MICHAEL AND CHARLOTTE GREEN** were ready for a new adventure. When visiting a friend in Portland, Oreg., who lived in a condo on the Willamette River, they spotted a floating-house community on the other side and became intrigued. Soon afterward they went driving around exploring floating-house communities. When they found one close to a nature preserve and a 20-minute bike ride to downtown Portland, they contacted their friend and one-time neighbor on Bainbridge Island, architect Russ Hamlet, for help.

Together they decided to first design a floating guest cottage, or a tender, as Russ calls it, to see if living in a floating cottage suited them and to give some of their design ideas a trial run of sorts. Happy with the results, they turned their attention to designing the main floating cottage that would be their primary residence.

Michael shared with Russ the inspiration he found in the aging waterfront warehouses they could see from the ferry going to and from Seattle and Bainbridge Island, where they had lived. It was important to Michael that the design of the floating house differed from what you might find in a "land house," as he describes it. He was looking for something with an industrial, loft-like feel, washed with daylight. And he was taken with the simple massing of old waterfront warehouses that had a primary central space featuring clerestory windows above flanking support spaces. Michael and Charlotte also wanted privacy from neighbors to the sides and outdoor living spaces both front and back.

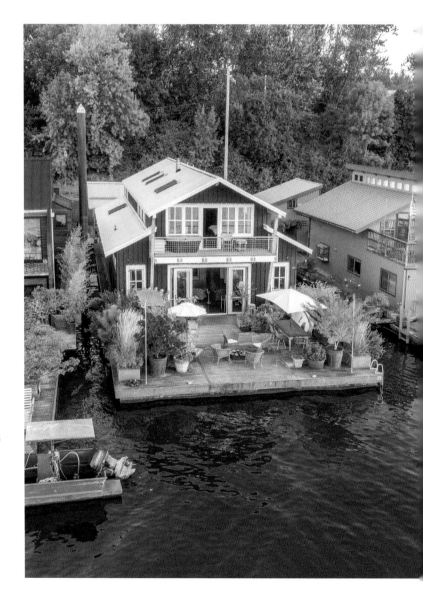

 The rear deck on the Greens' floating cottage (center) expands the living space toward the Willamette River and includes planters to incorporate a bit of the green vegetation, seen behind it, into the equivalent of their backyard.

  The floating cottage picks up on the simple massing of old waterfront warehouses and is accessed through antique gates salvaged from India, which lead from the community walkway.

**Architect: Studio Hamlet Architects**
Portland, Oreg.
**2,142 sq. ft.**

N

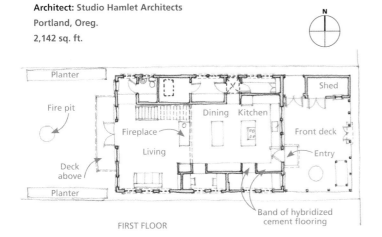

FIRST FLOOR

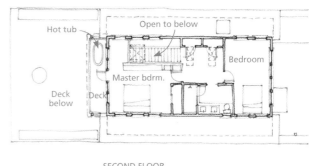

SECOND FLOOR

 A substantial east-facing, front-deck forecourt furnished for outdoor living offers a place to connect with neighbors. The cottage's roughsawn board siding was salvaged from the Columbia River. Russ refers to the siding installation as reverse board-and-batten.

The Greens' design goals, fire-code requirements for 2 ft. of exterior circulation space around the main house's perimeter, and other building envelope restrictions meant that Russ's design would need to pack a lot into a compact footprint. His multipronged solution addresses the access walkway with a sizable front-deck entry court that is enclosed with slatted boards to provide some privacy without blocking potential interactions with neighbors. Planted containers, both inside the courtyard and along the walkway, as well as an airy, salvaged entry gate topped with a rooflet, help uniquely engage their floating cottage with their floating-house neighborhood.

A large rear deck takes full advantage of both direct access to the Willamette River and the view across it, further engaging the cottage with the site.

For the cottage itself, support spaces are contained beneath human-scaled, one-story, sheltering shed roofs. They flank the sides of a two-story central gabled volume that contains the mostly open kitchen, dining, and living space on the first floor and the bedrooms on the second floor. The resulting simple massing recalls the waterfront warehouses that originally captured Michael's imagination.

Glulam beams and braces support a sheltering roof extension over the rear balcony off the master bedroom. Industrial-inspired galvanized corrugated roofing is visible from below. The roofline steps down to the one-story side shed roofs, contributing to the cottage's human scale.

The western, river-facing deck is a great place to enjoy sunsets, the fire pit, and dinner al fresco. A variety of furnishing vignettes lend the deck scale and comfort.

   From the entry, the semi-open plan offers an expansive distant view out to the river. A see-through gas fireplace—clad in hybridized concrete—and an open-framed stair made of stained Glulams, provide spatial definition without crowding the space or blocking the view to the rear deck.

   The kitchen has easy access through a French entry door to the breakfast deck and includes hybridized-concrete work counters, a nod to the concrete float beneath them. A simple and practical galvanized steel pot rack that Michael made hangs over an island finished with a galvanized top that includes a downdraft cooktop.

Exposed, stained Glulam joists support floorboards that provide the ceiling below. The 7-ft.-tall human-scaled partitions that contain side support spaces also accommodate built-in shelving and provide wall surface for the homeowners' eclectic art collection. Floors are primarily reclaimed Douglas fir.

Support spaces along the sides include a pantry, walk-through closet, mechanical room (which includes an efficient water-source heat pump, a sustainable feature that utilizes the river as a heat sink), powder room, laundry/sewing room, and small office. Seven-ft.-tall partitions separate the support functions from the 9-ft.-tall central living space. High side windows draw daylight into the support areas and beyond into the central living area while preserving privacy from neighbors. The contrast of the narrow, modest volume of the side spaces and the larger, taller volume of the main living area is a good example of how opposite spatial experiences can complement each other.

The wall of glass doors (both fixed and operable) toward the western waterfront deck on the first floor admit abundant afternoon light, while a French door and adjacent windows welcome generous morning light into the kitchen, all of which is augmented by the more indirect light streaming in from the high side windows. The result is a sunny and inviting common space. Upstairs, the bedrooms enjoy daylight from three sides, including a French door in the master bedroom leading to a small balcony overlooking the view. In addition, skylights above the upstairs landing help draw folks up the stairs and also illuminate the hall closet area.

The master bedroom is open to the stairs for a more spacious loft feel. Skylights over the stairway also brighten the bedroom. The same galvanized corrugated material on the roof appears below insulated rafters as a ceiling finish and reinforces the simple, industrial palette while providing surprisingly good acoustic properties because the corrugations bounce the sound around.

## A BIT ABOUT FLOATING HOUSES

Unlike a houseboat, a floating house is moored semi-permanently and doesn't have a means of self-propulsion. According to Russ, floating-house communities in Portland date back to the 1950s and 1960s and were seen as an alternative solution to finding an economical building site. Floats were cobbled together out of old-growth logs, and the houses atop them were generally one story. Fast-forward to the '80s and the popularity of floating houses increased as they came to be appreciated as a viable way to live on the water fairly inexpensively. In the next decade, some of the log floats began rotting, so folks began patching and replacing sections as necessary with Styrofoam, since old-growth logs had become hard to come by and very expensive as a result.

Michael and Charlotte Green's cottage is supported by a state-of-the-art concrete float that weighs approximately 208 tons and is made up of 26,000 lb. of rebar and 98 yd. of concrete. It was constructed by Marc Even of Even Construction, who also constructed the cottage. Concrete floats are very low maintenance and expected to last for decades, which makes them more sustainable than floats made of logs. Michael and Charlotte's float was custom engineered by a firm in Vancouver, B.C., and constructed in St. Helens, Oreg., where it was launched and where the rest of the cottage was constructed. Once completed, the cottage was floated up the Columbia and Willamette Rivers and ultimately put in place in the couple's community.

Michael and Charlotte purchased their slip and are part of their community's homeowners' association, through which they receive access to utilities and services like garbage removal as well as dredging approximately every 10 years to remove silt that can wash under floating houses. The slips are fairly close together, which contributes to the sense of community. A floating house isn't for everyone, but for adventurous spirits who are community minded like Michael and Charlotte, it's just the thing.

In keeping with the warehouse aesthetic, electrical conduit, galvanized ducts, and some framing is exposed. Floor joists overhead in the main living area are Glulams, an engineered laminated product. Russ called for them to receive a light blue-gray stain to tone down their inherent yellow color, so they would recede more. Walls are plaster. Bedroom ceilings upstairs are galvanized corrugated material like the exterior roofing. Floors in the service and entry areas are hybridized concrete to evoke the hardworking concrete float that supports the cottage. The bulk of the remaining floors are reclaimed Douglas fir, which lends a nice patina. Decks are durable ipe. The limited, consistent palette reflects the economy of means that typically characterizes cottages and adds to the informal somewhat industrial feel.

Living in their floating cottage has indeed proven to be an adventurous departure from a more conventional land house. Michael notes, "It's a lifestyle that we never experienced before. It's the best-kept secret." Plus, says Charlotte, "It feels like a vacation home."

   The master-bedroom balcony sports a custom hot tub that Michael fashioned from a Chinese tub made of cypress. He applied a clear fiberglass finish to the interior and painted the exterior. The galvanized hog-wire guardrail is fairly transparent, so it doesn't detract much from the stunning view while continuing the industrial theme.

# PERCH POINT

| ENGAGED WITH SITE | HUMAN SCALE | SIMPLE MASSING | SHELTERING ROOF | ECONOMY OF MEANS | INFORMALITY | SUNNY DISPOSITION | WABI SABI | CRAFTED DETAIL |

**A SITE WITH SIGNIFICANT SLOPE** is always a challenge, yet it can also present a great opportunity. This property on the North Atlantic in Biddeford, Maine, includes a bank rimming the coast about 15 ft. below and road access at the elevation of the top bank. To the northeast, it overlooks a spectacular but fairly narrow view corridor out to sea. Both the homeowner, Rick, and his architect, Caleb Johnson, wanted to take advantage of the ocean view while shielding the view of a neighbor's house to the southeast. There had been a rundown house, which Rick estimates was constructed in the 1960s, on the lot in approximately the same area when he acquired it, but it had been oriented differently.

*Natural materials outside and inside befit the coastal Maine setting.*

Perched on a rocky bank well above the North Atlantic, the cottage's simple cross-gable massing with human-scaled wings is oriented toward the prevailing view. An economy of white-cedar wall shingles, and cypress trim and detailing will weather gray, a color and finish characteristic of hardy coastal Maine. New plantings of native species help settle the cottage into the landscape.

 A prominent entry recessed into the front gable greets those arriving via the stone footpath off the street-level parking area as well as those who climb the stairs from the two-car garage tucked mostly out of sight beneath the cottage. The gentle bow of the white-cedar shingle wall of the front gable softens its countenance.

**Architect:** Caleb Johnson Studio
**Interiors:** Nicki Bongiorno
Biddeford, Maine
2,500 sq. ft.

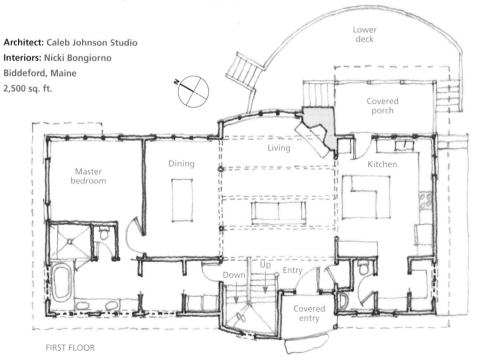

FIRST FLOOR

To best site the new dwelling, Caleb's design would need to address three often controlling issues: view, car access, and kitchen placement. In response to the ocean view, Caleb cranked the cottage to the northeast and pulled it back slightly from the water so that the main living areas could open onto outdoor living spaces, stepping down and engaging grade within the preferred view corridor. The dramatic slope meant that he could locate a two-car garage beneath the cottage toward the neighbor on the southeast end. Those arriving from the lower-level garage and those arriving from the street-level parking area share a common entry hall thanks to the side-by-side placement of the interior stairs and covered entry porch in the front cross gable. Locating the kitchen just steps from the entry off the living area makes it convenient for both day-to-day grocery unpacking and informal gathering, which is often centered around food prep and sharing.

Balancing the kitchen on the southeast end of the cottage is the master suite on the northwest end of the first floor, both

Caleb was sure to provide multiple layers of enclosure, going from the kitchen, for example, out onto the porch beneath a sheltering roof, down to the open, elevated, guard-rail edged curved deck, and, ultimately, groundward to the soft lawn of the outdoor living area bordering the rocky coastline.

The waterside porch, protected by an eastern white cedar–finished ceiling beneath the sheltering roof, includes crafted, cypress rafter tails. "I think exposing structure is a pretty cottagey thing to do" says Caleb.

   The open main living area boasts bright daylight and stellar views out the slightly bowed window bay as well as out similar windows in the dining area. Caleb located a granite-blend, angled fireplace in the corner so as not to hinder the view.

under human-scaled, grounding one-story roofs. Since Rick and his significant other, Ingrid, plan on retiring to the cottage in the not-too-distant future, accommodating first-floor living was a priority. The second-floor, within the simple, cross-gable massing, includes two guest bedrooms and a study beneath the sheltering roof. A side roof deck off the study and a small roof deck lookout over the living area bay below help extend outdoor living beyond the second floor too. A full bathroom and stair hall round out the second-floor spaces.

Both Rick and Caleb were particularly interested in using natural materials outside and inside that befit the coastal Maine setting. They opted for an economy of naturally weathering cypress trim and detailing in addition to white-cedar wall shingles to wrap the exterior. On the interior, accents of white oak add warmth and texture to the consistently light-colored walls with white trim. Custom-crafted, white-oak tapered columns receive exposed Glulam beams

  As in the dining area, a Glulam beam helps indicate the transition to the kitchen. Here, the tapered white-oak posts are a greater distance apart, allowing for an even easier, informal flow between the two spaces. A white-oak ceiling adds warmth and intimacy, as it does in the dining area.

in the open, informal living area and help define the different activity areas of dining, living, and kitchen. The turned, tapered-column shape, according to Caleb, is a result of creating a wooden column that has the majority of its mass where it's most needed structurally—in the middle. Caleb believes in an aesthetic that communicates structural performance and function. "I'm confident that if I'm honest about forces and materials then it will be beautiful," he explains. White-oak ceilings in the kitchen and dining areas further differentiate and warm those areas, lending them greater intimacy.

A slightly curved bay of windows extends the living area toward the view and picks up on the subtle curve in the plan at the front entry. A more sweeping curve edges the lower deck. "A curve in the floor plan, especially on a deck or patio, really lets you relate to the view and place your furniture in any fashion you want," notes Caleb. Ganged, large Andersen casement windows with transoms above partially wrap the

 Crafted, tapered white-oak posts receive a Glulam beam, signaling the transition to the dining area, which was located on the far side of the open space so as not to interfere with the more frequent use of the living area and kitchen. The dining area also provides a quieter buffer to the master suite.

   Windows in the first-floor master bedroom are sized like those in the living area, allowing the bedroom to visually expand outward and the view and daylight to wash in. The same white-oak floors and white trim help unify the spaces.

 In lieu of additional overhead cabinets, windows, which partially wrap the corner, come down to the counter to maximize view and daylight. Supplemental storage is provided by a pantry on the street side of the kitchen.

water-facing, first-floor spaces and flood them with daylight. Caleb isn't a believer in window muntins, which are often associated with more traditional architecture. As an alternative, he placed transom windows above casements to provide a transitional divided-lite look; this also allowed him to use more human-scaled windows (which are easier to manage) than if the casements had been the full height of the overall opening. Caleb particularly likes casement windows for the unobstructed view, light, and ventilation they offer and because when wind blows against them, it tightens their seals.

Rick and Ingrid delight in how comfortably the cottage lives and how casual it is. The flow from the indoors out onto the covered porch, down to the lower deck, and ultimately to the waterside lawn is particularly successful. "This building is very respectful of the site it was built on, the material that it's built of, and nature—all of which are important to a cottage," Caleb summarizes.

 Ingrid's study occupies a dormer under the sheltering roof and enjoys direct access to a side roof deck overlooking the cove.

# MOUNTAIN MUSE

ENGAGED WITH SITE • HUMAN SCALE • SIMPLE MASSING • SHELTERING ROOF • ECONOMY OF MEANS • INFORMALITY • SUNNY DISPOSITION • OPPOSITE COMPLEMENTS • WABI SABI • CRAFTED DETAIL

CHAD AND MANDY YONKMAN moved their family of four only a 15-minute drive south of where they had been living in Vermont, but it was a big move. They left behind a larger house with a two-car garage in a more populated area to live in a new, smaller cottage that they had custom designed and built in the Mad River Valley closer to friends, the schools their teenage kids attend, and their preferred mountain ski and snowboard destinations. Chad, a product/accessory designer with years of experience designing bags and now gloves, had always wanted to design and build a new house. He and the couple's architect, Elizabeth Herrmann, see a parallel between designing efficient bags with a pocket and place for everything and designing an efficient small cottage where no space is underutilized.

*An efficient small cottage where no space is underutilized.*

Gently settled on a small clearing, the quiet, dark, all gray exterior palette contributes to the simplicity of the cottage's massing. Morning light picks up on the texture and grain of the rugged barn boards. Fog adds to the mystery of the dark facade.

 A long footpath from the deliberately remote parking area leads to a step and stoop composed of two large stones found on the property that complement the dark linear siding. The gable-end facade with quiet, straightforward window apertures conveys the essence of cottage simplicity.

 The east-facing deck extends just far enough over the slope to accommodate outdoor dining and sitting but no so far as to require a guardrail and appear overly tall. Mandy notes that the property is private enough for her to enjoy doing morning yoga on the deck.

   Daughter Willa and Cosmo the pup enjoy the open living area's large-scale windows, which offer a stunning view and ample daylight. A glass door provides additional daylight and direct access to the deck. (Pedro, the cat, missed his photo op.)

   The woodstove is located to serve multiple areas. Countertops beyond are Formica on 1-in. Baltic birch plywood with exposed ply edges. Never fear: Items that aren't suited for display on the pristine open shelves can find a home in the pantry cabinet next to the refrigerator (not shown).

 Chad worked closely with the millworker to design clean-lined, simple cabinetry based on the layout Elizabeth provided. Flush, full-overlay MDF cabinet fronts with minimal finger pulls and open shelves supported by custom steel brackets of Chad's design create a quiet, open backdrop to the dining and living area. Chad made the 1-in.-thick Baltic birch plywood tabletop slab that rests on minimal trestles from Hay of Denmark, creating an airy dining arrangement.

FIRST FLOOR

**Architect: Elizabeth Herrmann Architecture + Design**
Fayston, Vt.
1,120 sq. ft.

Accessed from a lengthy winding driveway that skirts wetlands, the Yonkmans' cottage sits on a relatively flat section of a knoll within a clearing on the eastern slope of the Green Mountains. They deliberately elected to create a substantial distance between the car parking area and the house so as not to crowd the house, leaving it room to breathe and engage with the site. They elected to orient the cottage north–south so that a long deck on the east side overlooks a stunning view.

They knew they wanted a barn-like shape with simple massing, "something modern but that felt right in place with the aesthetic of the property and Vermont in general," notes Chad. So they opted for a 12/12 sheltering roof pitch and rough-cut, vertical barn-board siding. Their taste for Scandinavian design informed their selection of a single, dark-gray color for the exterior siding, window cladding, and metal standing-seam roof. It also influenced the interior light-colored palette of all white walls and ceilings, and Vermont ash sapwood floors most everywhere, except the

 Chad also made the stair hall's custom desktop out of the same Baltic birch plywood he used to make the dining tabletop. The hairpin legs are reclaimed. The exposed woodstove flue, notched into the desktop, becomes a hall accent feature rather than a boxed-in encumbrance. Because of the wide window swath and hall mirror, Mandy says, "You kind of feel like you're in the forest when you're sitting there."

entry-area mudroom and half bath. The predominantly monochrome interior palette contributes to the fluidity of the spaces, and the drywall finishes are affordable. Elizabeth notes that the palette also relates to the colors and textures of seed pods found in the wilderness. "They might be really rough on the outside and then you open them up, and they might have this smooth, light interior that almost takes your breath away," she says.

Both the Yonkmans and Elizabeth concluded that an open informal plan would make the best use of the small, budget-driven footprint. Plus, "Their family hangs out together and interacts, so it makes sense for them to have it pretty open," Elizabeth explains. Another advantage of it being open is that the shared spaces of the kitchen, dining, and living area can all borrow daylight and view from each other out large-scale windows into the mountain woods. Elizabeth chose sizable, mostly operable windows to connect the inside with the outside and vice versa, visually expanding each into the other. The jumbo-sized window in the living area isn't operable, but it's right next to an operable door. Elizabeth notes that she was "really trying to make big, large framed views and use the exterior almost like art, in a way."

Before breaking ground, Elizabeth, the Yonkmans, and the builder sat down with a consultant from Efficiency Vermont to work out the specifics of the building envelope and HVAC systems and equipment. They elected to insulate the 2×6 stick-frame exterior wall cavities with 3½ in. of closed-cell foam and wrap the outside of the exterior walls with 2-in. polyisocyanurate (polyiso) rigid insulation beneath a

## EFFICIENCY VERMONT

Established in 2000, Efficiency Vermont is a centralized statewide efficiency utility focused on energy conservation. Funded by a volumetric charge on all Vermonters' electric bills and additional funds such as those collected from the Regional Greenhouse Gas Initiative and the ISO New England Forward Capacity Market, Efficiency Vermont provides a variety of services, education, and incentives. It promotes the reduction of future power purchases and reduction in the generation of greenhouse gases,

limiting the need for upgraded transmission and distribution infrastructure and minimizing electricity costs. It serves residential, commercial, and industrial energy consumers.

In the case of homeowners, the scope of Efficiency Vermont's offerings range from rebates for appliance upgrades for Energy Star models to new-house efficiency certification and incentives. The first step is often an energy assessment. Chad and Mandy Yonkman received invaluable consulting

advice from Efficiency Vermont in determining the specific nature of their new cottage's building envelope and systems. They chose to implement many of the consulting engineer's recommendations and to pursue Efficiency Vermont's Residential New Construction certification. Once the cottage was determined to have met the standards for certification, Chad and Mandy received an incentive check.

 Wide tongue-and-groove boards painted white and installed horizontally provide a textured accent wall without adding distracting color or adding much to the budget. The small and lean Morsø woodstove contributes a nice contrasting color and element as does the hearth composed of six pieces of honed absolute black granite. Chad says they burn only 1½ cords of wood a year to heat their efficient home.

Elizabeth specified an extra-large operable tilt-turn egress window from Logic for the master bedroom. This window, like the rest in the cottage, is untrimmed except for an ash sill so as not to distract from the view. The sheltering roof lends the room coziness.

rain-screen system. They also installed 2 in. of Thermax poly-iso rigid insulation on the inside of the full basement walls and 3 in. of extruded polystyrene (XPS) rigid insulation under the slab. (The unfinished basement is used for utilities, storage, and their son's drum set.) Upstairs, the unvented cathedral ceiling is insulated with 2 in. of polyiso on the underside of the 2×12 rafters and dense-pack cellulose in the rafter bays.

The cottage is heated primarily with the woodstove, which was sized to be small enough not to overheat the efficient dwelling. There's an air-source heat pump mini-split, with one head above the couch, that provides supplemental heating when necessary and cooling in the summer. A heat-recovery ventilator (HRV) captures heat from conditioned stale air it exhausts and transfers it to fresh air it supplies; the

water heater also uses an air-source heat pump. Their laundry machines are electric too; the dryer is a condensing unit with a heat pump. They chose all electric-powered systems because they expect to install a solar photovoltaic system in the future.

"I love knowing that [our cottage] is really well built and built right and that it's going to be here, assuming after we're not around anymore that the next people love and take care of it, and the people after them love and take of it. It should be around for a couple hundred years," says Chad. Meanwhile, he and his outdoorsy family can enjoy their wilderness cottage.

 A small desk area, featuring a top constructed like the kitchen countertop, has a western view and is tucked into the open living area, providing a personal-scaled pocket for privacy. Chad and Mandy say the desktop has also become a landing pad for the phone charger/base, cell phones, and cell signal booster.

# AN ARTIST'S LAIR

| ENGAGED WITH SITE | HUMAN SCALE | SIMPLE MASSING | SHELTERING ROOF | ECONOMY OF MEANS | INFORMALITY | SUNNY DISPOSITION | OPPOSITE COMPLEMENTS | WABI SABI | CRAFTED DETAIL |

ARCHITECT CHRIS BARDT IS A PROFESSOR in the architecture department at the Rhode Island School of Design (RISD), as he was 28 plus years ago when I first started out at the school and was fairly mystified by conceptual design. He's also a principal at 3SIXØ Architecture, where he and project architect Jack Ryan designed this cottage in the woods for artist Allison Paschke. Together, the architects in collaboration with their client hatched a project you might find at a RISD critique—but built in the real world for a real client.

A connection to the ever-changing landscape.

   Large boulders excavated on site and relocated to offer structure to the garden set the stage for the simple massing of the cottage, itself faceted like a stone. The woodstove chimney is expressed to the left with a narrow projecting volume. Openings, like the one for the gang of glass doors, are mostly large, but kept to a minimum.

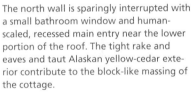 The north wall is sparingly interrupted with a small bathroom window and human-scaled, recessed main entry near the lower portion of the roof. The tight rake and eaves and taut Alaskan yellow-cedar exterior contribute to the block-like massing of the cottage.

 The tall window rising to the peak on the east face of the cottage floods daylight into the loft area above the utility room, which is accessed via the crafted, hidden, exterior door clad in the same Alaskan yellow cedar as the rest of the building. Stepping-stone-like decks, also constructed of Alaskan yellow cedar, accommodate outdoor living and will weather a silver gray with time, adding wabi sabi appeal, like the landscape itself.

Perhaps the most striking feature of the cottage is the simple massing of its form. The architects have come to describe it as crystalline. It started with a sketch by the artist client that was half opaque and half glass, as Chris describes it. Allison notes it was part living space part greenhouse, saying, "So the concept would be to really be one with nature, as much as possible." It was also important to Allison that it be small, no larger than a two-car garage, and that it be a cottage not a cabin. "I didn't want it to be doilies, or that kind of cottage," she clarifies. Chris was familiar with Allison's aesthetic because 3SIXØ had designed a double loft project for her and her husband in Providence. He and Jack appreciated that her woodland dwelling would need to express a refinement more often associated with a cottage than a cabin. Hers would be a weekend retreat from the city, primarily a gardening destination in Foster, R.I.

The architects set about creating small study models to suit the site, which included an old farmer's stone wall and a couple of natural clearings in the woods that weren't too far from the access road. They initially explored somewhat elongated forms that were bridge-like or linked with a wall, but came to realize that a compact form, closer to a cube, was better suited to such a small building. "By cutting the cube on the angle, it opened up a whole bunch of possibilities of exposing certain faces much more, creating low areas and high areas. With one step, you could have a lot of things happening," explains Chris. You could create spatial variety with nearby opposites that complement each other, creating local contrast. They then tweaked the models further to resolve how the roof, the expression of the chimney, and a large skylight over a bed nook could come together in a unified whole.

Chris and Jack knew early on that they wanted the main entrance to be located near the low portion of the building. There they carved a recess into the crystal-like form to create a sheltered entry that relates to human scale. Jack detailed the roof so it would have a tight eaves and rake to help the cottage read as a multifaceted form wrapped in Alaskan yellow cedar rather than as roof-capped walls. A cascade of strategically placed rain diverters on the roof over doorways helps protect them. The feeling of a sheltering roof, in this case,

 The recessed opening quietly announces and shelters the entry. It occupies, in theory, what the architects refer to as the thickness of the wall. Once beyond it, those inside find themselves under the lower end of the cathedral ceiling in the main room, so the transition from compression to its opposite, and complement, expansion isn't too abrupt.

 An arbor constructed where the slatted western red cedar fences overlap provides a gateway to the entry paths; the cobblestone option forks right toward the informal deck entry, and the crushed-stone option winds around toward the more hidden main entry.

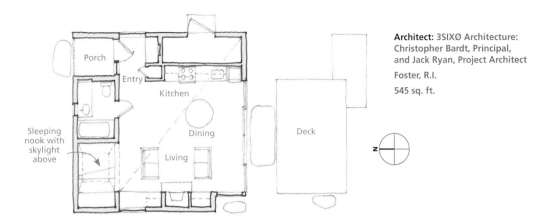

Porch

Entry

Kitchen

Dining

Living

Sleeping nook with skylight above

Deck

N

**Architect:** 3SIXØ Architecture: Christopher Bardt, Principal, and Jack Ryan, Project Architect

Foster, R.I.

545 sq. ft.

The informal living area feels light and airy thanks to the volume of the sheltering roof, abundant daylight, and spare yet warm palette. The nested alcoves offer more intimate opportunities to participate in the larger space, while being somewhat removed from it.

Daylight and view are celebrated beneath the sheltering roof via large windows and ganged glass doors that engage the site by visually bringing the outdoors in and extending the experience of those within the open room out into the landscape. The southern view continues beyond the deck, and nearby salvaged boulders, out to the patio that Allison and workers pieced together from enormous rocks unearthed during excavation.

comes not from a roof overhang but more from the form of the roof from within.

The architects sited the cottage so the roof soars toward the southeast, ensuring that large windows and glazed doors would capture daylight and a view of the old farmer's stone wall and a meadow beyond, making them part of the interior experience. Allison's interest in Japanese garden design influenced the landscaped approach—from the southern parking area to the north side of the cottage—which integrally engages the cottage with the site. Those arriving wind between two custom, overlapping, vertical-slatted, western red-cedar fences across a small footbridge and can access a stepping-stone shortcut to their right, toward the more informal glass-slider entry or they can continue ahead on a crushed stone path that wraps around the building to the more formal, and a bit more mysterious, main entry.

The idea of the singular form evident on the exterior is expressed on the interior as a single open room beneath a dynamic cathedral ceiling, with alcoves that are meant to be understood as occupying the thickness of the walls. The walls and ceiling of the informal primary room are finished with painted white tongue-and-groove pine boards installed with a gap to allow for expansion and contraction as well as to add texture. They're contrasted by the crafted, clear-finished

The IKEA-cabinet kitchen outfitted with custom doors sits in a Douglas fir niche that backs up on the utility space. A ladder, not shown, can be mounted on pins at the opening in the rail to gain access to the sleeping loft under the sheltering roof.

Douglas fir niches of the entry alcove, kitchen, and desk/shelving area. Matching Douglas fir also appears as flooring running diagonally in the direction of the ridge, reinforcing the sheltering sloped planes overhead. The muted gray of the cabinet faces, refrigerator, and plaster woodstove surround complete the quiet palette, which expresses an economy of means. "The cottage gains strength and even size by being singular in its conception and its execution," explains Chris.

The contemporary aesthetic of Allison's cottage feels very current but so, too, does its connection—visually through glass expanses and physically in its siting—to the ever-changing landscape and Allison's gardens. She continues to work her property, planting and nurturing native woodland plants in the quiet amid the clean, fresh air of the woods. "Those things make me feel like I'm really a constructive integral part of the land and its creatures," she says. It looks to me like her cottage is a constructive and integral part too.

 A large skylight in a pyramid-shaped shaft above the bed nook creates a personal observatory at night and sunlight catcher by day. "That sleeping loft is about where gravity goes away," says Chris.

 The sizable 4-ft. by 8-ft. window in the Douglas fir desk niche aligns with a window of the same size off the entry, so you can stand in the entryway and look left or right and see straight through the building to connect with the landscape. The sleeping nook features the same style and color cabinets as in the kitchen, continuing the succinct palette.

# TWO VIEWS

ENGAGED WITH SITE    HUMAN SCALE    SIMPLE MASSING    SHELTERING ROOF    ECONOMY OF MEANS    INFORMALITY    SUNNY DISPOSITION    OPPOSITE COMPLEMENTS    CRAFTED DETAIL

*Inside, each part sings out to a different thing.*

IT'S NOT UNCOMMON FOR A DWELLING to address a notable view by lining up parallel to it, but what to do when there are two distinct compelling views to experience in different directions? The property on Washington's Hood Canal that Diane and David Bowe acquired for their getaway posed just such a question. To the south, beyond a meadow in a clearing, is an expansive view out to Hood Canal. To the west, from high up on the bank, there's a view through a tree line that drops off to an inlet and beyond to the snow-capped Olympic Mountains. Now, factor in the request for a getaway design inspired by the modest sommerhus, or summerhouse, vernacular of Denmark that Diane, a first-generation Dane, made of her architects, Geoff Prentiss and Dan Wickline.

Situated on a high bank above Hood Canal within a clearing of Douglas firs, the Bowes' cottage expresses muted, human-scaled simple massing beneath steeply sloped sheltering roofs, much like a Danish sommerhus.

   Three cedar decks at floor level spill from the cottage into the landscape, expanding informal outdoor living toward different view experiences. The dark, painted cedar, reverse-board-and-batten siding in combination with the dark standing-seam metal roof suggests an economy of means and aims to meld the cottage with the surrounding treed landscape.

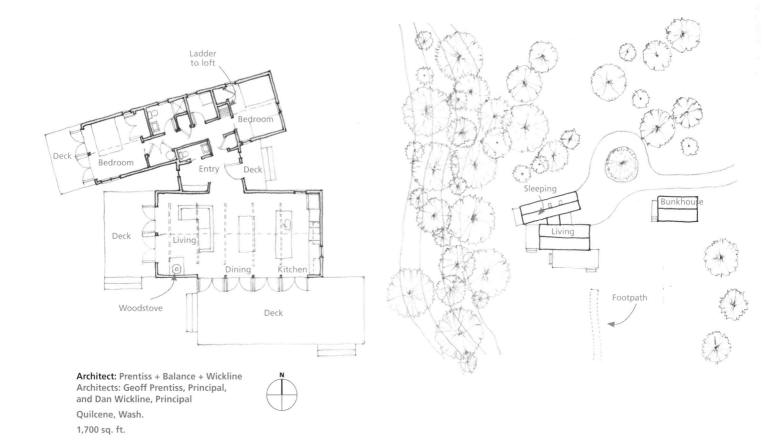

**Architect: Prentiss + Balance + Wickline Architects: Geoff Prentiss, Principal, and Dan Wickline, Principal**

Quilcene, Wash.

**1,700 sq. ft.**

Geoff and Dan were undaunted. They proposed dividing the active and quiet spaces of the cottage into two distinct human-scaled, narrow, one-story, steeply gabled volumes—like Danish summerhouses—linked by a low, flat-roofed connector. "When you have these steep gabled forms, you really don't want a building that's too wide, because you end up with something that feels like a barn," explains Dan. They arranged the simple massing such that the quiet gabled volume that contains the bedrooms, a sleeping loft, and bathroom is nestled up against the trees to the north with its short end oriented toward the quiet vista through the trees and to the western mountains. They pulled back the slightly wider, active gabled volume of the kitchen/dining/living area—allowing some southern exposure for the master bedroom too—and oriented the long side parallel to the active view to the south, over the meadow toward the footpath leading down to Hood Canal. The placement of the two components engages the site's unique view opportunities and preserves the meadow. A third gabled volume that's a bunkhouse edges the top of the meadow. It was a scrappy structure on the property when the Bowes acquired it; they renovated and relocated it.

The two simple gabled forms are slightly offset from each other and cranked in relation to each other to create a funneled approach in between, leading to a flat-roofed entry connector. Repeated skinny windows facing away from the views are the same proportion as French doors facing the views, creating harmony between the different apertures.

Four pairs of aluminum-clad French doors off the active kitchen/dining/living space open onto a deck, bringing the outdoors in and the indoors out. French doors offer more open access than conventional sliding doors, in which half the opening is closed, and are more affordable than many other types of glazed doors for large openings.

 The sunny kitchen/dining/living area is open to a sheltering cathedral ceiling that is 18 ft. above the floor at its peak. Contrasting dark collar ties—each crafted of two steel plates with a 1½-in. space in between—cleverly conceal wiring and an inexpensive track for a variety of light fixture types. The ties also lend scale and rhythm.

   The light-colored, economical, pine plank floors are also found in the bedroom wing and relate to the pine windows and doors, trim, and open shelves in the kitchen. The dark, relatively affordable, sustainable Richlite island top (made of resin-infused paper) picks up on the dark accents of the collar ties, pendants, some furnishings, and other items throughout the cottage.

From the dining table and kitchen, the view out the French doors across the deck, out to the meadow, beyond the footpath, and ultimately to Hood Canal below is exhilarating and expansive.

Entry into the cottage occurs between the two gabled forms in the flat-roofed connector. Because the active kitchen/dining/living volume is pulled away from the quiet sleeping volume, it helps catch approaching guests and funnels them toward the entryway. The quiet volume is cranked toward the main, active volume just enough to create a wide, welcoming entry area. "You're drawn into the entry of it. And when you're inside, each part sings out to a different thing," says Geoff. The wedge shape of the connector, in plan, also suits the modest mudroom toward the apex. The ceiling in the entry/mudroom is a compressed 8 ft., which complements the feeling of release experienced beneath the 18-ft.-tall ceiling (to the ridge) in the cathedral ceiling space of the active volume.

The dark, informal reverse-board-and-batten exterior with a dark metal standing-seam roof and contrasting bright, light interior are another aspect of the Danish influence. Diane and David painted the cedar siding with Benjamin Moore's Black Panther themselves. "The dark exterior helps it blend into its surroundings," notes Dan. An economy of white Sheetrock walls and ceilings; light-colored, wide-plank pine floors in the living and sleeping areas; and grounding slate on the entry floor, beneath the woodstove, and on the master bathroom floor keep the interior simple and cohesive. Multiple ganged French doors flood the kitchen/dining/living area and master bedroom with daylight. They also bring the outdoors in and indoors out, seamlessly expanding informal living space onto the three decks that are at the same level as the interior floor. The cathedral ceilings beneath the sheltering roof in the main active volume, as well as in the master and guest bedrooms, also contribute to the interior airiness.

Much like the Danish cottages that inspired the Bowes' new cottage, Diane notes, "It's a place to go and unwind and enjoy people." Although the intent is similar, the design is updated. Geoff adds, "It looks sort of urbane, and clean, and nice, but there's nothing really precious about it. You can trudge right through and use it all and feel comfortable." Ultimately, the Bowes' new cottage aspirations were simple: "A place like this should bring you joy, and it does," says Diane.

 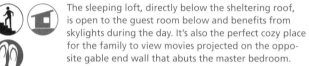

The sleeping loft, directly below the sheltering roof, is open to the guest room below and benefits from skylights during the day. It's also the perfect cozy place for the family to view movies projected on the opposite gable end wall that abuts the master bedroom.

The master bedroom also enjoys a sheltering cathedral ceiling. The quiet view out the French doors and through the tree line to the west is peacefully serene, which suits the sleeping wing of the cottage. The finishes pick up on those in the kitchen/dining/living wing and help unite them.

The sitting area focuses on the quiet view to the west through the tree line. A Danish RAIS woodstove is a primary heat source. The slate beneath the stove and the dark stove itself, complete with its dark flue, pick up on the contrasting dark accents of the collar ties and other dark elements.

# AMONG THE TREES

ENGAGED WITH SITE | HUMAN SCALE | SIMPLE MASSING | SHELTERING ROOF | ECONOMY OF MEANS | INFORMALITY | SUNNY DISPOSITION | OPPOSITE COMPLEMENTS | CRAFTED DETAIL

A three-season retreat from the city.

ED NEUBAUER AND I WERE ARCHITECTURE CLASSMATES at the Rhode Island School of Design (RISD). We were both older students with previous degrees who had been bitten by the design bug a little late in the game. Like many who come to something late, we had a fervent curiosity about our newly chosen undertaking. Twenty-five years later at our class reunion, we discovered our overlapping interests had continued beyond RISD to include a passion for cottages.

Upon arrival through the woods, the driveway opens to the small clearing that Julia's saved trees delineate. The cottage's simple massing nestles gently into the landscape.

White-cedar shingles speak to its Maine location, while a large classical column and modestly sized double-hung windows contribute to a traditional look.

   From the south side, the screen porch is visible beneath the sheltering roof that brings the eaves down to human scale. The fire pit is prepared to be lit at sunset, and Jake the dog has already claimed his fireside spot.

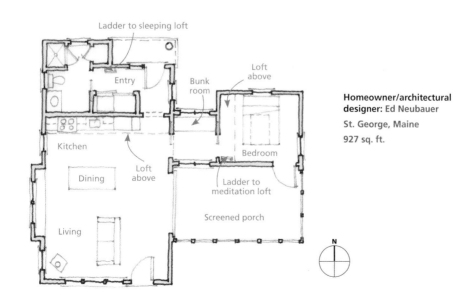

**Homeowner/architectural designer: Ed Neubauer**

St. George, Maine

927 sq. ft.

Initially trained as an educator, Ed had developed a side interest in renovating his homes. In the 1980s, the step-father of his now wife, Julia, sensed that Ed was ready to take on a more formidable building challenge and asked him to construct a new post-and-beam house for him in Maine. Ed signed on, agreeing to exchange his labor for land. As a result, Ed ended up with a 2½-acre parcel in the woods behind his patron's house. And there the wooded land sat, not only while Ed attended RISD but for a total of about 25 years. Then one summer, while Ed and Julia were walking the wooded property not long after Ed had been laid off from a gig, Julia made a pronouncement: either they build there now or sell the property. In short order, Ed designed a cottage that would serve as the family's three-season retreat from the city and refuge from the hubbub of their Maine community.

They found a promising building site—not too far from the right-of-way that gave them access to the lot—that was relatively flat and wasn't hindered by "motions," which Ed describes as protruding chunks of granite that are considered small quarries and are typically worked on-site to form pavers. Next, "Julia became the tree queen," as Ed describes it. She marked trees with blue tape that were to be saved, delineating the general area of the future cottage and the winding driveway that would offer intermittent glimpses of the cottage to entice and engage those approaching.

Working with a tight budget, their modest cottage took on a simple, one-story, T-shaped form with sheltering gable roofs that contribute to its human scale. Julia's sense of Maine's typically more traditional cottage exteriors influenced their choice of medium slopes for the roofs; white-trimmed, white-cedar shingles; and the Doric-like single column at the entry to their cottage. Double-hung windows with divided lites in the top sash add to the traditional look, yet circular windows punctuating the peak of the primary gable ends hint at something else.

While Julia had been helping hold Ed's "RISD impulses" (as we call them) in check with respect to the exterior of the cottage, they allowed themselves more freedom inside the cottage, shaping a fresh, more current, unconventional

 A wall-mounted, clear-finished pine ladder provides efficient access to the skylight-lit sleeping loft above the front entry and service area. Clear-finished pine trim around the openings off the entryway dress up the spare, white Sheetrock walls and ceilings elsewhere in the cottage.

 Ed and Julia generally close the glass-paneled garage door between the living area and screen porch during Maine's cool summer evenings, but open it during warmer summer days to welcome breezes and expand the living space toward the outdoors. During the brisk shoulder seasons it's generally closed but still admits abundant daylight.

  The open dining and living area beneath the cathedral ceiling is an informal, sunny, multi-purpose space. Stainless-steel tie rods, which Ed had fabricated, and a steel Morsø woodstove offer clean industrial accents to the crisp, unadorned interior aesthetic.

 Ed crafted the sleeping loft guardrail out of Baltic birch plywood newels, steel tubing, and leftover cable boat rigging that he had on hand. He made the dining table out of a hospital gurney that was being discarded; he topped it with Baltic birch plywood and added a Baltic birch plywood storage bin below.

The warm, clear-finished maple cabinets; pine band trim and baseboard; fir garage door; and Baltic birch plywood dining set balance the cool grays of the concrete floor, stainless-steel appliances, table gurney, cable guardrail, and steel tie rods. A mirror over the sink allows whoever is washing dishes to look at a reflected view out the south windows.

living space. Because creating experiences of compression and release for those moving through the small cottage was important to Ed, he designed a lower ceiling at the compact entry and service area that complements its opposite, an open cathedral ceiling in the kitchen/dining/living area. Not wanting to waste space, he designed a sleeping loft to inhabit the sheltering roof above the entry area for their then-seven-year-old daughter. He took a similar approach when he compressed the ceiling in the bunk room and transitioned to a cathedral ceiling in the adjacent master bedroom, which contains access to a meditation loft within the roof above the bunk room.

Revealing the concrete slab via gridded polished concrete floors and finishing walls and ceilings with minimally trimmed, white Sheetrock throughout the cottage communicate an economy of means, while also setting an informal stage for cottage living today. Having ganged the bathroom, laundry, and kitchen wet wall together for reasons of budget and ease of construction, the plan sets up an informal sequence of circulating upon arrival through the open kitchen area en route to the dining and living areas beyond. A glass French door to the south that aligns with the glass entry door draws occupants through the space toward daylight and view, which also contributes to a legible space.

The screen porch off the living area is accessed by a glass-paneled overhead door. When it's open, the informal living space appears to double, visually, and there's even greater access to daylight. "We're most often in the landscape right there on the screen porch, no matter what the weather is, because it's open and exposed to the outside," says Ed.

Ed and Julia had been clear from the outset that they planned to create a cottage, not a cabin. "A cottage has a sort of air, light, crispness—a contemporary feeling to it," remarks Ed. He also associates the idea of cottage with summer. He further notes, "It has that elegance to it." Now that it's complete, he and Julia couldn't be happier with their new cottage. "It feels very magical, very special," says Ed.

From within the cathedral ceiling area of the master bedroom, it's possible to see the meditation loft over the adjacent bunk room. A skylight adds to the appeal of the loft space beneath the sheltering roof. A scored line in the concrete floor subtly accents the view axis straight ahead through the west-facing window.

When the garage door is up, inside and out blur and the living space expands significantly. Because one-story living and accessibility are important to Ed and Julia, the screen porch slab is continuous with the living area slab. The 4-ft. by 4-ft. grid scored into the slab lends it scale and reinforces view and procession direction.

Ed constructed the built-in window seat of pine. The lower ceiling over the window bay complements the cathedral ceiling of the living area. The window seat offers a pocket to tuck into with a book or game.

# BARN HYBRID

ENGAGED WITH SITE · HUMAN SCALE · SIMPLE MASSING · SHELTERING ROOF · ECONOMY OF MEANS · INFORMALITY · SUNNY DISPOSITION · WABI SABI · CRAFTED DETAIL

A PARCEL OF LAND CONTAINING A BARN without an accompanying dwelling could easily be overlooked by some house hunters, but Kathleen and Peter Fitzgerald recognized a good find when they came across it. "We both love barns," notes Kathleen. The barn in question sat alone in a field surrounded by cascading conservation land in Freeport, Maine. Intrigued by the listing, Kathleen and Peter invited their architects Rob Whitten and Jessie Carroll of Whitten Architects for a look. All agreed, the property had exciting potential, so Kathleen and Peter acquired it.

> Because the windows are so big, you're immediately drawn to the outside.

Due to the one-story, human-scaled simple massing of the cottage addition, the barn's gable roof can accommodate solar panels on its southeast face, which is mostly out of sight from the road and approach. Stonework in the form of a hefty walking path, entry terrace (featuring a reclaimed millstone), and low wall engage the house with the site.

 The rear of the house includes multiple-level terraces with different vantage points and degrees of intimacy that help mitigate the site's dropping grade. The cottage's oversized windows invite the indoors out into the landscape.

  A shallow entry porch beneath a sheltering roof extension off the cottage creates a perch for overlooking the extensive conservation land beyond and below. The white, reverse-board-and-batten siding hints at the Scandinavian influence on the cottage.

Because the architects generally like to design the approach to their projects from the north with the procession traveling toward daylight and primary living spaces to the south, the barn's positioning relative to the road to the northwest and conservation land to the south and southeast was perfect for locating an addition to the southeast. They worked with Kathleen, who's also a landscape designer, to further engage the barn and addition with the site. Kathleen elected to keep the existing informal dirt driveway and enhance it with reclaimed cobbles and river stone in front of the barn garage doors. Then, using substantial reclaimed and Maine-quarried stone, she shaped walls, pathways, and terraces that casually flow out and step down from the structure toward the approach and the conservation-land view.

To capture the soul of the late-1800s cottage that Kathleen had been living in for 23 years before acquiring the barn property with Peter, the architects proposed wedding a modest one-story, human-scaled, gabled cottage addition perpendicular to the gabled barn. The addition would house an open-plan living area and wide entry service hall. The barn, which had been constructed of structural insulated panels (SIPs) and reclaimed beams about 10 years earlier, would accommodate a first-floor master bedroom suite beyond two car stalls; beneath the sheltering roof on the second floor they planned an office and guest living space. The simple massing of the resulting T-shaped form is in keeping with the New

 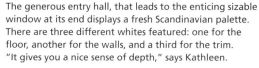

The generous entry hall, that leads to the enticing sizable window at its end displays a fresh Scandinavian palette. There are three different whites featured: one for the floor, another for the walls, and a third for the trim. "It gives you a nice sense of depth," says Kathleen.

## ARCHITECT WENCHE SELMER AND NORWEGIAN SUMMERHOUSES

Wenche (pronounced Vehn-keh) Selmer's career spanned 44 years in which roughly half of her commissions were coastal summerhouses or mountainside cabins; the other half were single-family residences. Launching her architectural practice in 1954 in the midst of the male-dominated mid-century Modern movement, Wenche's work deliberately took on a more domestic tone, focusing on small dwellings for family living connected to their natural settings and informed by modern spatial concepts. For 12 years she also taught at the Oslo School of Architecture, first as an assistant professor and then as an associate professor.

Summerhouses of her design were characterized by their simplicity, relationship to their natural environment, respect for Norwegian vernacular tradition and materials, as well as appreciation for modern fluidity and daylighting. Local spruce and pine figure prominently in her work, in addition to some natural stone and varied expanses of glass. Gable roofs, or "saddle roofs" as they are sometimes known, were common features of Wenche's summerhouses, though she also experimented with some lower-sloped shed roofs. The clarity of her work, its simple massing, straightforward hardy materials, rigorous—often open—plans expressed in playful relationship to the surroundings continue to inspire me today. As a female architect who started my residential practice at about the age Wenche started hers, also working out of my home and with an interest in educating, I'm thankful for the career she forged more than a generation ahead of me and the groundwork she laid for my own.

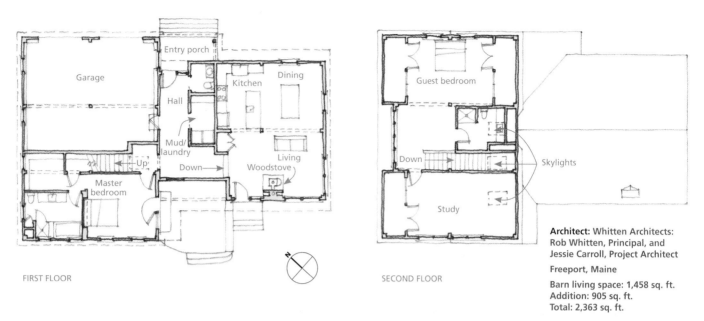

Garage

Entry porch

Kitchen

Dining

Hall

Mud/laundry

Up

Down

Living
Woodstove

Master bedroom

FIRST FLOOR

Guest bedroom

Down

Skylights

Study

SECOND FLOOR

**Architect:** Whitten Architects: Rob Whitten, Principal, and Jessie Carroll, Project Architect

Freeport, Maine

Barn living space: 1,458 sq. ft.
Addition: 905 sq. ft.
Total: 2,363 sq. ft.

The living area includes a Shaker style Wittus woodstove venting out a whitewashed brick chimney with side recesses just deep enough to house fireplace tools. The oversized double-hung windows were a more economical alternative to ganging multiple units in the same overall openings. They welcome abundant daylight inside and visually expand the living space out into the landscape.

The random-width, rustic, white-oak flooring and crafted hemlock timber frame add wabi sabi character to the Scandinavian palette of the open living space, which provides a quiet backdrop to showcase some of the furnishings Kathleen has collected. The addition is heated primarily with radiant heat floors.

England tradition of connecting dependent volumes over time to a primary structure.

The project also took on a Scandinavian sensibility. For design inspiration, Rob had shared with both Kathleen and Jessie a book about the work of Norwegian architect Wenche Selmer, who happens to also be my own architectural idol (see p. 126). The reverse-board-and-batten cottage exterior of the addition, in which the board and the batten exposure are equal, riffs on similar economical treatments found on the understated, simple cottages of the late 1950s and 1960s that Wenche designed on the coast of Norway. "It established this rhythm at a scale that's accessible, trying to not call your attention to one or the other," explains Jessie.

A new, exposed, hemlock timber frame constructed within the budget-sensitive, stick-built addition (which includes roof trusses) relates the interior of the open-plan living area in the addition to the barn interior. It was crafted to include pegs like those in the barn frame. The original plan had been to stain the new timber frame to resemble the original timber frame of the barn, but when the owners and architects saw the inherent light color of the new rugged hemlock once it was installed, they agreed it better suited the Scandinavian palette left natural and also helped differentiate new from old, while adding wabi sabi appeal.

When considering how the homeowners would use the cottage and barn, the architects understood that Kathleen and

Kathleen sourced reclaimed marble for much of the kitchen countertops and backsplash, which express natural texture and the patina of use. Reclaimed marble stair treads serve as shelves in the island. The soapstone sink is also salvaged. In a nod to the landscape outside, the base cabinets are dark to ground them and the upper cabinets are white to suggest the lightness of the sky above.

The open living space is two steps below the entry level, which allows for a taller 10-ft. ceiling that lends the modest footprint expansive airiness. A soapstone hearth relates to the soapstone sink. The stairs to the upper-level office/sitting room and guest quarters in the barn are on axis with the window that was behind the photographer who took this shot.

 The master bedroom is on the first floor within the barn, where it has direct access to a small patio dedicated to it. The reclaimed, rugged, dark timber frame provides a nice wabi sabi contrast to the pristine, white plaster walls. A white board-finish wall accents the custom recess for the headboard and side bookshelves.

Peter would need a transition space between the garage portion of the barn and the open-plan living space. Their solution was to introduce a wide hall between the two that serves both as an entry space from the driveway and garage and also accommodates the service spaces of a mud/laundry room and half bath. An oversized double-hung window at the end of the hall opposite the front entry invites southwestern daylight and offers view of the landscape, enticing those arriving to approach it. Once there, the journey continues to the left down two steps into the 10-ft.-tall volume of the living/dining/kitchen area. There, oversized double-hung windows and a glass door to a rear stepped terrace wash the space with daylight and provide views in multiple directions. "Because the windows are so big, you're immediately drawn to the outside . . . I never get tired of that," says Kathleen.

The cottage's open-plan living area and wide entry hall, as well as the barn's first-floor master suite and upper-level office/sitting area off the guest quarters beneath the sheltering roof provide a satisfying variety of spatial experiences. "We don't need huge rooms. We purposely designed this with Rob and Jessie to fit our lifestyle for where we are in our life right now," concludes Kathleen.

 Upstairs in the barn beneath the sheltering timber-framed roof, the partition between the office/sitting area and the guest quarters stops short of extending to the ridge. This allows the adjacent uses to visually borrow space from each other. The painted floor, as in the entry hall, is budget friendly and provides some relief from the clear-finished white-oak floors found elsewhere.

# CAMPINOTTAGE

ENGAGED WITH SITE · HUMAN SCALE · SIMPLE MASSING · SHELTERING ROOF · ECONOMY OF MEANS · INFORMALITY · SUNNY DISPOSITION · OPPOSITE COMPLEMENTS · WABI SABI · CRAFTED DETAIL

THE LINE BETWEEN A CAMP, A CABIN, AND A COTTAGE can be somewhat blurred. That certainly seems to be the case with this small getaway in the woods of Johnson, Vt., within earshot of a tributary of the Lamoille River. How a getaway is used, in combination with its location and characteristics, can help determine where on the camp/cabin/cottage spectrum it falls. Rick and Martha, clients of the Cushman Design Group, had this off-the-grid campinottage designed and built on a parcel that's part of the Vermont Land Trust, a little over a half-hour drive from their Stowe vacation house. They had an approximately 1-mile-long access road constructed in order to reach it, which is no small task; they keep an all-terrain vehicle garaged at the road's entry so that they can reach the campinottage no matter the weather.

*A clean, more modern interpretation . . . of a rustic camp.*

Perched on piers, the simple massing of the shed form includes a sheltering roof with deep overhang toward the entry at the lower, human-scaled eaves. Vertical shiplap hemlock siding will weather to gray over time to become more in sync with the dark-gray bonderized corrugated accent finish, ultimately blending in with the surrounding tree trunks.

On the eastern river side, the sheltering shed roof soars. The dark gray bonderized steel emphasizes the roof shadow line and is a modern take on a durable material.

**Architect:** Cushman Design Group
**Architectural Services:** Chad Forcier and Kelley Osgood

Johnson, Vt.

830 sq. ft.

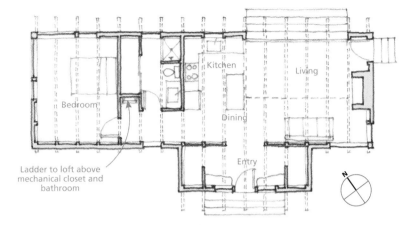

Bedroom

Kitchen

Living

Dining

Entry

Ladder to loft above mechanical closet and bathroom

N

 When open, the large overhead Haas Door invites the outdoors into the lightly whitewashed wood interior. The ebony-colored aluminum finish on the door adds a modern industrial touch as does the crisp steel hearth and surround on the Stûv fireplace, contrasting the textured wood it complements.

The open living/dining/kitchen visually expands into the wilderness when the overhead door is open. The interior feels like a screen porch when the LaCantina horizontal rolling screen-door system in the large opening is engaged.

Still, it's not the get-lost-in-the-vast-woods kind of cabin that Rick had originally imagined he would have built in the Northeast Kingdom, where he might go stream to stream looking for optimum fly-fishing conditions. Instead, Rick and Martha use their getaway for a variety of outings, including fly-fishing, hiking, and mountain biking, and as a diverting destination for hors d'oeuvres and cocktails with friends around the fire when they're visiting their vacation house in Stowe. "It's more of an integral experience with our other property because it's close," explains Rick. So perhaps their getaway's lack of extreme remoteness and its use for a variety of limited-duration activities moves it a bit away from the cabin end of the spectrum.

Due to the challenging property access, significant excavation for concrete foundation walls wasn't an option, so the campinottage treads lightly on preconstructed concrete piers. It sits on a high bank in a small, relatively flat clearing among a stand of hemlocks. A rear deck facing east engages the roaring sounds of nearby waterfalls pouring into the river gorge

that's out of view. Rick deliberately chose to site the structure a fair distance from the river's edge so as not to disturb it. "Aesthetically, I didn't want to mess it up because it was too beautiful," he notes.

Rick along with Chad Forcier and Kelley Osgood of Cushman Design Group settled on the shed-roof simple massing early on in the design process. "I like the open design of the interior that it affords," says Rick. In addition, the design team likes that the sheltering shed roof rises and opens toward the river. The form also lends itself to the uncomplicated, exposed, hemlock timber frame and hemlock sheathing "outsulated" with structural insulated panels (SIPs). What might have been a very campy or cabin-like warm knotty-wood interior receives a bit of cottage refinement in that the wood isn't heavily knotted, and all of it, except for the ash floors, received a light whitewash finish.

When the budget didn't allow for a screen porch, the design team had the idea to install an exterior screen system paired with an overhead door off the living area instead.

 A slatted window seat made of the same hemlock as the undersized timber bents provides a human-scaled niche to take in the view of landscape and provides wood storage below. Don't miss the bear decor.

  Kelley, who is also a fly-fisherman, proposed that the typically exterior finish of cedar shingles be applied to the interior of the chimney mass, seemingly bringing the outdoors inside. That's a brown trout, which is highly sought after locally, integrated into the shingle finish.

 The sheltering shed roof rises toward the eastern wall in the direction of the river. Contemporary horizontal muntins in the French door play off the horizontal rails in the large glass overhead door.

"You lift it up and you feel like you're out on a screen porch," says Kelley. The somewhat industrial feel of the aluminum overhead door and the raw steel fireplace surround move the getaway further from the rustic camp or cabin vibe toward the direction of a more refined cottage for today. "This whole project was based on doing a clean, more modern interpretation," notes Chad. Oversized windows and glass doors with horizontal muntins further contribute to the contemporary aesthetic and enhance the connection to the wooded site while washing the interior with daylight. Outfitted with a single bedroom, full bath with improvised loft sleeping above, and an informal open living/dining/kitchen space, the campinottage is purposefully small and efficient.

It's served by a septic system, draws (very tannic) water from a spring well pump, and utilizes a zero-clearance, wood-burning fireplace for heat as well as auxiliary wall heaters. Electricity is provided by a bank of car batteries that were initially solely charged by a propane-fueled generator and has since been augmented with a solar photovoltaic charging system. Such refinements also nudge it more toward being a cottage than a roughing-it, rustic cabin.

Be that as it may, Rick and Martha have had fun outfitting the getaway with campy decor, like the carved-bear lamps on the couch end tables and curious fishing-themed art work. No matter what you call the getaway, "It's got this whole other thing going on around it driven by the river," says Rick. It's more than a campinottage; it's part of the landscape.

  The low eaves of the sheltering roof at the entry provide a human-scaled transition space. Waning-edge benches, crafted by the contractor from a tree that fell on his own property, add a cabin slant to the consistently whitewashed hemlock frame and hemlock wall and ceiling boards.

   Large corner windows connect the bedroom with the landscape and morning daylight. The contractor made the woodsy bed, which puts the "camp" in campinottage.

  The open kitchen/dining area includes informal, open base cabinets made of the same hemlock as the structure, also whitewashed. Open upper shelves help the kitchen corner integrate with the overall open space rather than appear as a mass within it. Utilitarian light fixtures feature utilitarian exposed conduit, which furthers the informality of the campinottage interior.

# AT THE BASE OF THE BUTTE

ENGAGED WITH SITE    HUMAN SCALE    SIMPLE MASSING    SHELTERING ROOF    ECONOMY OF MEANS    INFORMALITY    SUNNY DISPOSITION    OPPOSITE COMPLEMENTS    WABI SABI    CRAFTED DETAIL

ONLY A FEW YEARS AFTER HE and his future wife, Cheryl, had taken up cross-country skiing, Jason Quintana picked up an in-flight magazine during a business trip and learned of extensive cross-country ski trails in Washington's Methow Valley. It was serendipity. That summer, he and Cheryl took a long weekend in the area to explore. "Instead of mountain-biking around on the trails like we planned to do, we mountain-biked around looking at for-sale signs," he says. The vacant parcel they found and ended up acquiring backs up

*Maximizes connection to the outdoors, daylight, and view.*

At the base of ponderosa pines and firs climbing toward a butte, Jason and Cheryl's cottage also overlooks a soft meadow, above which it appears to hover. A low-slope, sheltering roof tops the human-scaled, simple massing.

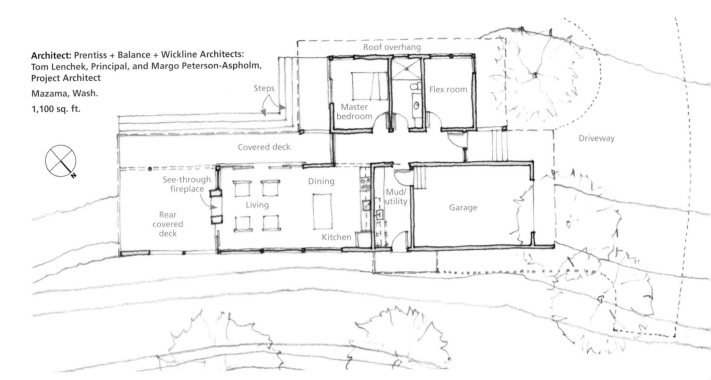

**Architect:** Prentiss + Balance + Wickline Architects:
Tom Lenchek, Principal, and Margo Peterson-Aspholm,
Project Architect

Mazama, Wash.

1,100 sq. ft.

Roof overhang

Flex room

Steps

Master bedroom

Driveway

Covered deck

See-through fireplace

Dining

Rear covered deck

Living

Mud/ utility

Garage

Kitchen

   The outdoor living spaces off the kitchen/dining/living wing, bedroom/flex room wing, and hall are sheltered by the broad overhanging shed roof, which "folds" over to become the long north-east wall. Glass on both ends of the hall contributes to its indoor–outdoor breezeway-like feel.

Continuous ipe stairs, which will weather gray and mesh with the charcoal-gray metal and wood siding, lightly descend to the meadow, making access easy, informal, and gracious. The color palette inside and out picks up on the colors of the site.

to national forest and is across the street from a hub of trails maintained by Methow Trails, a non-profit. Their lot is part of a development that requires dwellings be no smaller than 1,000 sq. ft. "Small is what we wanted," Jason notes. More specifically, something around 1,000 sq. ft., all on one floor that feels larger, and with outdoor living. Oh, and with somewhere "indoors and dirty" for ski gear, a small metal shop for Jason, and a pottery studio for Cheryl.

Architects Tom Lenchek and Margo Peterson-Aspholm set to work creating a couple of schematic designs for their clients to consider. Ultimately, Jason and Cheryl selected a scheme that orients the cottage with its long axis nearly parallel to the forested steep butte at the rear of the property to the northeast and locates the cottage such that it nudges the base of the butte. This allows the cottage to capitalize on a

southwest exposure overlooking a meadow, which it engages toward the front of the property.

To maximize connection to the outdoors, daylight, and view, the architects divided the spaces into a smaller, narrow bedroom/flex room/porch wing and a longer, slightly wider, open, informal kitchen/dining/living/porch wing. They separated the two parallel private and public wings, in part, with a hallway that feels like a breezeway. They further attached a mudroom/utility room and multipurpose "indoors and dirty" space for a car, gear, and hobbies in line with and toward the kitchen end of the public wing. The two wings are positioned so that one slides past the other.

The open living area wing is closest to the butte. Within it, the dining/living/porch areas enjoy daylight and views in three directions. The more private wing bumps into the

The indoor/outdoor gas fireplace from Heat & Glo is faced with steel, which has acquired a patina in places that resembles the warm plywood tone. The outdoor living area complements its opposite indoor living area. Continuous plywood finishes on both help tie the indoor and outdoor spaces together, expanding both in the process.

The charcoal-gray, standing-seam metal of the roof that "folds" onto the exterior wall facing the butte suits the northeast exposure in the snowy climate. The openings where the wall partially encloses the outdoor living area frame views, welcome breezes, and invite soft northern daylight.

meadow, and both the bedroom and flex room enjoy daylight and view in two directions. A low-slope sheltering roof, rising to the northeast in the direction of the forested butte, caps both human-scaled wings (including attached outdoor spaces), as well as the hall in between, creating simple massing.

The architects then introduced an economy of materials to reinforce their design concept of two parallel wings and an in-between interstitial space, each visually expanding onto covered outdoor spaces. "We like clean; we don't like a lot of detail in everything," says Jason. "Having materials that have interesting looks to me is the detail . . . . Carrying those interesting-looking materials from inside to outside also makes the house feel a lot bigger," he continues.

Those materials include a charcoal-gray, standing-seam metal roof that "folds" down to become the exterior vertical siding on the northeast side of the longer wing closest to the butte. The same material makes an appearance inside on the southwest side of the hall, stopping just above the door frames. The other side of that hall is finished in the charcoal-gray-stained, rough-cut, horizontal fir siding that extends on the outside of the exterior walls that don't include a metal finish on one side. The exterior wall finishes on the interior of the hall, in addition to the concrete floor (which is found throughout the cottage) and full-height openings at both ends, convey an informal breezeway vibe.

Plywood makes an appearance both indoors and outdoors as well. It can be found on the opposite side of walls or roofs featuring metal finishes. Thus it's on the ceilings throughout, including on the underside of the sheltering roof, which projects over the decks of the two wings and the hall. And it's on the inside of the wall finished with metal on the exterior that edges the living area and the inside of the hall wall partially finished with metal that edges the bedroom/bathroom/flex room. Plywood adds warmth and texture and is a relatively inexpensive option that speaks to how modern buildings are constructed. The light color also relates to the color of the meadow grasses, just as the dark-charcoal color of the metal and wood siding relate to the bark of the ponderosa pines climbing the butte, further blurring inside and outside. "I like the contrast," says Jason.

The standing-seam metal finish, also found on the exterior, continues on one side of the breezeway-like hall above the cheerful yellow interior doors and frames. White-painted Sheetrock on the rest of that wall is more dog-friendly than the metal and brightens the space. Horizontal, rough-cut cedar from the exterior continues on the other side of the hall and reinforces the horizontal massing of the cottage.

 The simple galley kitchen of maple-veneer cabinets and open shelves along with a plastic laminate countertop is quietly efficient. Jason and Cheryl store some canned goods in the mudroom/utility room and use a sideboard for additional storage. The concrete, radiant-heat floor, which runs throughout the spaces, is informal, durable, and inexpensive.

In the living area, the gas fireplace is faced with the same steel finish as on the exterior, which adds continuity, texture, and visual interest. The full-height fir glass sliders, full-height windows, and transoms above allow the indoors and outdoors to blur together. Jason and Cheryl's mid-century modern furniture is right at home in their modern mountain cottage.

To keep the cottage bright and on budget, white painted Sheetrock on interior partitions and the inside of wood-finished exterior walls reflect the abundant daylight streaming in ganged glass doors, full-height windows, and transoms. Those apertures also reinforce the connection with the outdoors. The covered decks, which will weather gray, lightly tread on the meadow as does the bedroom/flex room wing, which cantilevers 2 ft. beyond its foundation toward the meadow, creating the appearance of floating above the grasses.

Now that the cottage construction is complete, Jason and Cheryl have plenty of time to enjoy the vast cross-country ski trails out their front door. They currently live in their Methow Valley cottage about 30 percent of the time and in their condo in Oregon about 70 percent of the time, but one day, they imagine they'll flip that ratio. They look forward to spending even more time in the cottage engaged with the Methow Valley landscape and its wildlife. Jason reports they've seen bears, moose, deer, coyotes, and, of course, birds there. They've even seen cougar prints in the snow behind the cottage. Someday they might see the cougar. Maybe it's a good idea to be careful what you wish for.

Though smaller, the bedroom boasts corner glazing—in the form of sliders and an equally tall fixed window—which helps the space feel larger, engaged with the site, and bright. The warm plywood sheltering ceiling begins its slope up from the human-scaled 8-ft. height of the southwestern exterior wall.

# IN A COMMUNITY

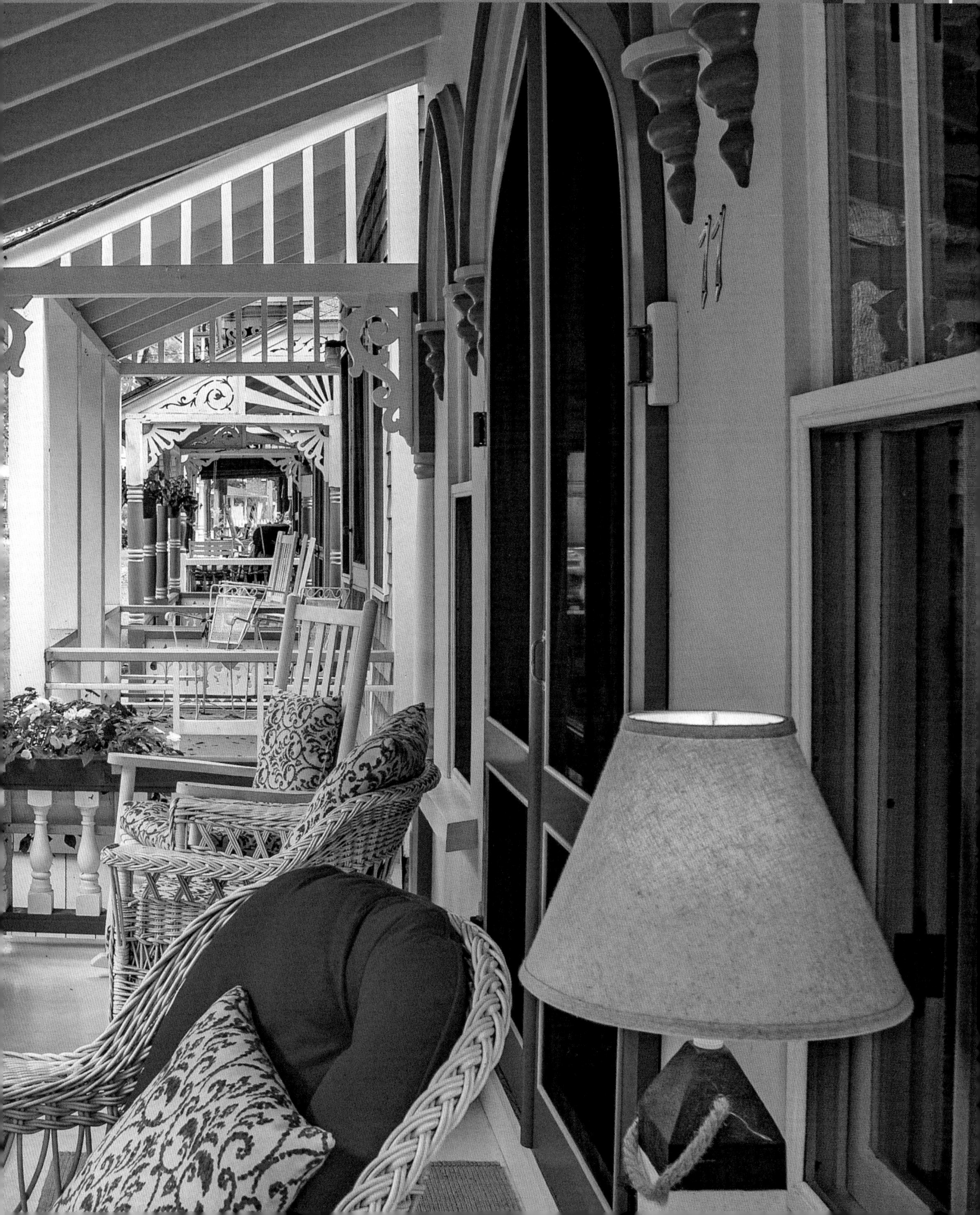

# SUMMER HEIRLOOM

ENGAGED WITH SITE · HUMAN SCALE · SIMPLE MASSING · SHELTERING ROOF · ECONOMY OF MEANS · INFORMALITY · SUNNY DISPOSITION · OPPOSITE COMPLEMENTS · WABI SABI · CRAFTED DETAIL

ONE FEBRUARY I RECEIVED A VOICEMAIL from Paul Bedard, a prospective architectural client in my neighborhood, who had recently returned from a ski vacation only to discover that the pipes had burst in the second-floor bathroom of his antique cottage and flooded the first floor. Despite news of such a grim event, he sounded surprisingly energized. "I needed that kick in the pants that was provided to me accidently by the pipes bursting," Paul now realizes. He had been pondering renovating and expanding his c. 1910 cottage for years, so when I first met with him on site, he was ready to dive into the design process.

The updated design respects the original character of the cottage.

  In the summer, Paul's prized hydrangea tree, which we were careful to save, hides the wrapping, enclosed porch-like addition on this simple massing. The original porch, tucked under the cottage's sheltering roof, was reconfigured so the entrance shifted toward one end, which made for larger seating groupings on the porch and in the living area.

The intimate scale of the front porch is accentuated by the playful swinging bench (which looks toward a glimpsed water view) and three small awning windows (which offer a bit of indirect daylight and a whisper of a sea breeze to the addition over the dining banquette).

From the side volleyball area, the exterior details of the human-scaled, enclosed porch-like addition are apparent. They include a lower shingle wall that aligns with the front porch guardrail wall and windows placed between pilasters that resemble the front porch posts. A flat-panel treatment below the kitchen casement windows suggests porch infill panels.

His cottage in our unique, seaside, former summer community in Rhode Island had been in his family since his great aunts Evelina and Clarina acquired it in 1930 as a summer getaway. Then in the 1970s, it passed onto his godmother, Aunt Elise. By 2001, it had fallen into a state of disrepair and was headed toward foreclosure, when Paul acquired it for his year-round residence. "I couldn't bear to lose it because of the history there," Paul says. So it was important to him that the updated design respect the original character of the cottage—including its simple massing, modest scale, and relationship to an open side yard—while adding bonus living space, reimagining the kitchen, and improving flow.

Situated on one side of a double lot, part of the cottage had long faced an open lawn that over the years had become home to an annual volleyball game tradition. Any addition

FIRST FLOOR

**Architect:** Katie Hutchison Studio
Warren, R.I.
1,794 sq. ft.

With the entrance shifted, the reconfigured living area easily accommodates a comfortable seating arrangement in front of windows relocated to welcome more southern daylight. The original painted floor joists above remain exposed, and new beadboard, supplementing the existing, was extended to wrap the living area. A new door on an informal barn-door sliding track leads to the back hall.

   The large opening between the original cottage and new addition gives the living area more breathing room and invites visitors toward the expansive sunny addition. The applied mahogany beams on the addition ceiling are an updated spin on the exposed floor joists overhead in the living area. The gas heating stove in the addition echoes the design of the woodstove insert in the living area's original stone fireplace.

would need to preserve the volleyball area. It would also need to mesh naturally with the compact neighborhood's informal, unassuming dwellings, which had mostly all started out as casual summer escapes. "I placed as much, if not more, importance on the outside of the home and what people's view would be before they even came inside," explains Paul. He also wanted to pay attention to capturing natural light and expressing structure and detail on the ceiling. To that end, he shared many inspiration photos with me of sunny screen porches and enclosed porches. This sparked the design solution.

I proposed what became a one-story addition that springs from the original front roofline and wraps the house to the north, intended to resemble an enclosed porch. The addition's

The space-saving custom banquette and table sit beneath the small two-lite awning windows that look out to the porch. The white channel-board wainscot that wraps the room is incorporated into the backrest of the mahogany banquette to integrate the two and creates a boat-like feel.

The ganged casement windows with divided lites in the kitchen are critical to creating the enclosed porch-like effect of expansive views and ample daylight. Soapstone counters, which will darken and gain more character with time, contrast the white, full-overlay, more contemporary look of the Shaker style base cabinets.

A warm, jatoba-topped breakfast bar, which will become a richer color with age and sun exposure, overlooks the kitchen and out the French doors toward the rear yard. The rhythm of the crafted mahogany beams overhead parse the open space, seemingly enlarging it.

The original light, square-stock balustrade facing the living-area side of the stairs is complemented on the addition side by baluster boards that are the width of the spaces between the balusters on the living-area side. The resulting guardrail is not only more solid but also creates a backrest for the new custom built-in bench whose seat aligns with the second tread.

Upstairs in the office beneath the sheltering roof, the expanded dormer adds needed headroom and daylight. The new awning windows are the same size and style as the single window that had been in the original dormer. The new beadboard finish helps relate the office to the beadboard in the central living area and stairway.

low eaves line lends it relatable human scale, and the continuity with the original porch roof helps integrate it, while maintaining simple massing. To keep from impinging upon the volleyball area, the addition is kept to a narrow 13-ft. width. A sheltering, cathedral ceiling with an applied mahogany beam treatment reinforces the addition's porchiness and suits an informal open kitchen and dining area. Windows that wrap the porch-like addition, as well as a pair of French doors that open onto a new rear patio, flood the addition with daylight and engage it with the site.

A built-in banquette adds a crafted touch while occupying less space than a conventional dining table wrapped by freestanding chairs. The original stairs, which used to descend along the exterior wall of the main room, are integrated into a large opening between the living area and the addition, allowing the living space to borrow visually from the addition and for the addition to feel part of the original cottage. A custom built-in bench along the stairs provides a special spot for guests to informally engage with the activity of the kitchen.

We acquired additional square footage by bringing a rear exterior porch and flanking outdoor utility closets—which had bordered the original kitchen and dining locations—into the building envelope. The combined reclaimed spaces were converted into a rear hall entrance with a laundry and full bathroom along one side and a new library/den/future bedroom on the other. Upstairs, we lengthened an original single-window rear shed dormer in two directions to become a five-window shed dormer that accommodates a larger office and reconfigured full bathroom.

Consistent finishes help connect the original cottage with the cottage it has become. On the first floor, newly installed reclaimed southern yellow pine resembles the patina of the original flooring, which was damaged by the burst pipes, and unites the addition with the original cottage. White, channel-board wainscot in the addition riffs on the beadboard in the original living room. Mahogany accents on the addition's ceiling beams pick up on mahogany in the dining banquette. Soapstone, which will become a rich, darker color over time with use, is found on the kitchen counters and makes another appearance as new hearth and mantel materials in the living area.

We walked a delicate balance to bring Paul's twentieth-century cottage into the new millennium. "It had to have elements that remind you of the way the home was—to trigger those memories—and maintain a simplicity. Expand and modernize but not go too far to lose sight of what it once was," remarks Paul. Sounds like a cottage updated for today.

# CAMPGROUND SALVAGE

| ENGAGED WITH SITE | HUMAN SCALE | SIMPLE MASSING | SHELTERING ROOF | ECONOMY OF MEANS | INFORMALITY | SUNNY DISPOSITION | OPPOSITE COMPLEMENTS | WABI SABI | CRAFTED DETAIL |

I REMEMBER THE FIRST TIME I visited and became smitten with The Campground on Martha's Vineyard when my family summered on Island in the 1970s. For Kathryn Allen, it all started with a Grand Illumination Night. She and her young vacationing family stumbled on the annual August event, in which the roughly 300 cottages of The Campground are festooned with

The reappearance of old finds . . . adds meaning, connection, and playful informality.

The cottage's 1½-story original primary gabled form is outfitted with a 1-story side bay and front porch that help ground it and contribute to the cottage's human scale. The new 1-story, gabled-roof form of the new full bath (on part of the former shed's footprint) complements—in a smaller and slightly less ornate way—the original house, picking up on finishes and porch post detailing. And the pocket courtyard garden adds charming outdoor cottage living space.

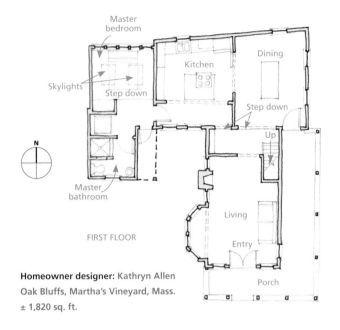

Master bedroom

Skylights

Kitchen

Dining

Step down

Step down

Up

N

Master bathroom

Living

Entry

Porch

FIRST FLOOR

**Homeowner designer: Kathryn Allen**
Oak Bluffs, Martha's Vineyard, Mass.
± 1,820 sq. ft.

No wonder Kathryn fell in love with The Campground on her first Grand Illumination Night, a tradition dating back to 1869. The paper lanterns warm the storybook cottage exterior with a dreamy glow. The gingerbread crafted details and finishes are hallmarks of The Campground's Carpenter Gothic style.

glowing colorful paper lanterns. "I just floated through that night. I thought this is the most magical experience I've ever had," she recalls. Fast-forward nearly 20 years, when Kathryn, no longer married, and her travel-writing daughter scheduled a trip to the island, planning to attend their first tour of The Campground cottages. As Kathryn puts it now, "I would say that's the most expensive tour I ever took," because while on it, she noticed there were 12 cottages for sale and was soon inspired to acquire one of her own.

Certainly, the sense of community and that magical Grand Illumination Night attracted Kathryn to her Campground cottage, but her passion for history and the cottage's unique siting were also big draws. Though the cottage and its grounds were in rough shape, the c. 1871 property had much to recommend it. Front bargeboards on the overhanging roof boast unique carved depictions of a hunter, a rabbit, and a pouncing dog; thus the cottage is known as "Hunter House"

or "Hare Hunter Hound." Kathryn couldn't resist such unique detailing among the many Carpenter Gothic features; what's more, the cottage's unusual (for The Campground) double lot afforded space for outdoor living within the embrace of the U-shaped footprint.

Kathryn and her fiancé, Dick Miller (whom she and her family refer to as Miller), have since enhanced those features and more. They laboriously scraped, sanded, repaired, and repainted the gingerbread detailing, which, unlike many homes in The Campground, continues around the side of the cottage. They created an intimate courtyard garden within the lot's open space, after first placing an underground dry-well in its midst to capture roof runoff. And with the assistance of architect Frank Pitts, they transformed the one-story flat-roofed attached storage shed—which makes up the third leg of the U-shaped plan—into a gable-fronted master suite that now deftly contributes to the cottage's legible massing.

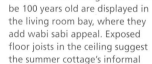

Tall Gothic Revival style windows and French doors with unique crafted casings add character while welcoming generous daylight into the fresh-white front living room. Five original paper lanterns that came with the cottage and could be 100 years old are displayed in the living room bay, where they add wabi sabi appeal. Exposed floor joists in the ceiling suggest the summer cottage's informal construction.

Large two-lite over two-lite double-hung windows march around two sides of the dining space, brightening and seemingly enlarging it. White beadboard wainscot and original crowned window casings within light-colored plaster walls offer a crisp backdrop for the dark patina of the room's furnishings, which include chairs that are original to the cottage and an ice chest (to the left) from the shed that Kathryn sanded and refinished, transforming it into a dining storage chest. She notes that since it's on wheels, they roll out the chest to the courtyard to cool drinks during parties.

 This custom vanity, eaves cabinet, and mirror were conceived by Kathryn and constructed by Miller. They're composed of salvaged components from a large old breakfront cupboard that the previous owners had in the dining room. The combination of ornate detailing contrasting a simple, flat background recalls the cottage's exterior treatment and is a good example—on a furnishing scale—of opposite complements. The colorful painted finish adds to its cottagey authenticity.

"Maintaining the historical integrity of the house was huge to me," Kathryn explains. But inside she wanted to remove the narrow hall of doors between the front living area and the back kitchen, understanding intuitively that the small cottage would feel larger and brighter if the spaces were open yet still distinct from each other. She planned to reuse the original glass-fronted kitchen cupboard and adjacent overhead cabinets but desired a more accommodating kitchen layout, so she moved the stove to an island and placed the sink in front of a resized window in a new run of cabinets that are sympathetic to the old. Kathryn also appreciated that by stealing space from a second-floor closet, which extended into the eaves, she would be able to accommodate a generous vanity in a reconfigured full bath. The recent changes she made converting the former shed to a master bedroom, laundry room, and full bath has rendered the cottage all that more livable for the five to six months of the year she and Miller are lucky enough to use it now.

Though the framing of the cottage walls and roof was no longer open when Kathryn acquired the cottage, she

 The informal bedroom under the steeply pitched sheltering roof is intimately scaled and feels surprisingly spacious in part thanks to the simple white walls and ceiling and to daylight entering from two directions. The pop of orange on the gable window casing, bureau knobs, and the bedspread reinforces the room's sunny disposition.

 These built-in, glass-fronted cabinets are original to the cottage; in them, Kathryn discovered the picture frames and china plates, now mounted on the either side of the kitchen window. She found the blue pedestal that receives the black honed-and-leathered granite island top at an antiques store in Troy, N.Y. It's a former altar.

The refinished original floor of the dining room and hall lighten the space and express some of the cottage's history. A cheerful blue, detailed screen door and hopper window off the wrapping porch add a punch of playful color, as does the apple-green stairway.

## THE MARTHA'S VINEYARD CAMP MEETING ASSOCIATION (MVCMA)

Originally a ½-acre Methodist camp meeting ground established in 1835 in the town now known as Oak Bluffs, worshipers gathered for religious revivals that could continue for days. By 1840, The Campgrounds grew to include 20 or so tents in a circle. Then in 1859 more substantial wood-framed, wood-sided, and canvas-topped "tents" were added to the mix. And in 1864 Carpenter Gothic wooden cottages began to make an appearance. By 1880 there were 500 cottages, some of which would later

be moved elsewhere on Island, merged with other cottages, or fall into disrepair and be demolished. Today, there are approximately 300 surviving densely sited cottages—the great majority of which are seasonal vacation homes— on 34 acres in The Campgrounds.

The MVCMA was formally established in 1860 with a 21-member board of directors, and it was incorporated in 1868. To this day, The MVCMA owns the property on which the cottages reside. A tabernacle in the center of The

Campgrounds was constructed in 1879 of wrought iron, which a campgrounder convinced the board of directors was less expensive than constructing it of wood. In December 1978, the MVCMA was listed in the National Register of Historic Places, and in 2005 it was declared a National Historic Landmark. The MVCMA oversees a vigorous architectural review process of proposed changes to the cottages.

was determined to keep the original flooring, exposed floor joists, and as much of the salvageable contents that came with the cottage as possible, both out of respect for the cottage's history and a certain economy of means. To that end, she repurposed bed headboards, a breakfront cabinet, antique china, picture frames, and other furnishings in unexpected and creative ways. The reappearance of these old finds, often reconfigured and repainted, adds meaning and connection for Kathryn and lends the cottage a playful informality. "I love a house that has surprises," notes Kathryn. Hers is chock-full of them. See how many you can spot in the photos.

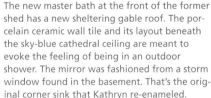

The new master bath at the front of the former shed has a new sheltering gable roof. The porcelain ceramic wall tile and its layout beneath the sky-blue cathedral ceiling are meant to evoke the feeling of being in an outdoor shower. The mirror was fashioned from a storm window found in the basement. That's the original corner sink that Kathryn re-enameled.

The master suite renovation of the former shed includes two different roof lines. The shed roof over the bedroom helps finesse the transition to the cottage's second story without compromising the windows at that level. Little hopper windows above the bed contribute cottage charm and a peek of daylight, which is supplemented by the large skylights overhead.

# CAMPGROUND REDUX

ENGAGED WITH SITE | HUMAN SCALE | SIMPLE MASSING | SHELTERING ROOF | ECONOMY OF MEANS | INFORMALITY | SUNNY DISPOSITION | OPPOSITE COMPLEMENTS | WABI SABI | CRAFTED DETAIL

Re-created elaborate gingerbread details . . . and a cottage interior for nearly year-round use.

WHEN ERIN AND RICH CUMMINGS acquired their cottage, its location in the Martha's Vineyard Campground was its primary asset. According to town papers, the original c. 1871 cottage in that location had burned to the ground in 1973. A new cottage, based on the original plans, had been built in its place in 1974, but, of course, most of the historic material was gone. This made some of Erin and Rich's renovation decisions easier, because changes wouldn't involve sacrificing original material. It also meant, however, that their cottage no longer had the original intricate gingerbreading depicted in an antique photo of the house that a campground historian shared with them.

The Saturday after they bought the cottage, while Rich went out to get coffee, Erin found a sledgehammer in a closet and knocked out one of the walls of the middle room that blocked the view from the back kitchen of The Campground green and Tabernacle. "I knew to leave the vertical studs; I knew that they had some importance," she laughs. Rich came back 10 minutes later and loved being able to see some of the circle from there. So they decided to knock out the other intervening wall of the middle room. They suspected that opening up the first-floor spaces to each other would better accommodate their informal Vineyard lifestyle and allow light to travel deeper into the cottage from each end.

 Bob Gatchell, known as the "Gingerbread Man," re-created the elaborate gingerbread details based on studying the historic photo of the cottage (facing page). The pint-sized upper balcony offers an opportunity to enjoy intimate proximity to the cottage and also the broader experience of The Campground below. It complements the sheltering, more contained space of the bedroom it adjoins.

This historic photo depicts the cottage in its early days, long before the fire of the '70s.

 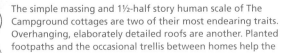  

The simple massing and 1½-half story human scale of The Campground cottages are two of their most endearing traits. Overhanging, elaborately detailed roofs are another. Planted footpaths and the occasional trellis between homes help the cottages engage with the site. The center balustrade at the Cummings' porch steps is removable, but is often in place to keep the family dog contained.

Their renovation goals were initially modest. They figured they would simply have the interior whitewashed the first year, then address the exterior, and, after living in the cottage for a couple years, determine what else they might want to do. But when painter Fred "Rick" Huss gave them an initial estimate to paint the interior of the then exposed plywood and framing of the walls and second-floor cathedral ceiling, he suggested they consider insulating the roof first, since the second floor could otherwise overheat in the dog days of summer. Erin and Rich then got to thinking: Why not insulate the walls while we're at it? And so it goes, one thing led to another. They decided to update the cottage interior for nearly year-round use and retain carpenters to re-create much of the original exterior detailing and then some.

Inside, Erin decided to finish all the walls and ceilings in a neutral palette, so the transitions between the different areas

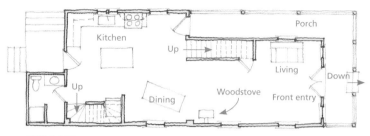

FIRST FLOOR

Homeowner designer: Erin Cummings
Oak Bluffs, Martha's Vineyard, Mass.
1,180 sq. ft.

  The close cottage porches offer a chance for neighbors to chat informally, while engaging the greater community of The Campground. Erin worked with her painter, Adalberto Silva, to carefully identify which surface would be which color in order to create greater apparent depth. The blues all come from one Pratt & Lambert color card with the lightest iteration on the porch floor and the second lightest on the porch ceiling.

  The dining area opens to the kitchen, with each borrowing space visually from the other. The warm patina of the aged hemlock floors and the other consistent elements of the simple palette make for a smooth transition between spaces. The Jøtul gas stove, on the left, can heat the first floor during the shoulder seasons.

  Pointed-top Gothic Revival French doors, common in the community, are said to be reminiscent of the parted curtains of The Campground tents of yore. Erin and Rich kept the floor joists exposed overhead as is typical of The Campground cottages' informal interiors.

  Colorful stained glass at the peak of the tall, pointed-top Gothic Revival windows that flank the entry doors is a uniquely crafted detail that contributes to the cottage's sunny disposition. The carpenters custom-cut the beadboard ceiling finish to fit in between the floor joists.

 With the spaces open to each other, there's enough breathing room in the kitchen for the table island that Erin chose for its simple distressed pine look. It, in combination with the textured woven chairs, complements the crisp, harder edges of the cabinetry and joists. The blue scrollwork over the sink is a remnant from the cottage's previously failing bargeboards, which Erin painted blue and distressed.

 Erin believes the round-top French doors of the master bedroom leading to the balcony came from the neighboring cottage, which also had been severely damaged in the '70s fire. The cathedral ceiling under the gable is simultaneously cozy and spacious, in part due to its geometry and height. Erin painted the bed, which came with the cottage, pink and distressed it down to its original green in places.

Erin and Rich picked up the horizontal leaded window when they found the two for the bedroom wall, but didn't know where they would put it. One of the carpenters surprised them with the perfect location. It lets daylight into the small full bathroom and acts as an interesting accent in the hall.

would be easy, allowing one space to blur into another to create a roomier feel. "We went a little beadboard crazy," she cheerfully notes. But beadboard seemed the right choice for the cottage vibe she aimed to create, and there was a certain economy to it. On the first floor, beadboard is applied as a wainscot for a dressier look. Upstairs, beadboard runs up the full height of the walls. Ceilings upstairs and down are lightly pickled, broader, select-pine beadboard, which has a warm glow. Erin took a similar approach to the floors, sticking with one material per floor to link the spaces. Aged hemlock floors—chosen in part for their contrasting warm hue— replaced the linoleum on the first floor, and more affordable refurbished oak floors were installed over the bare plywood on the second floor. Erin figured pops of color could come from the furnishings, which would allow her to change things up later if she so chose.

As for the exterior, the "Gingerbread Man" Bob Gatchell of Splinters & Sawdust Woodworking was on task. He rebuilt the gingerbread bargeboards on the overhanging sheltering roof to match the failing bargeboards, and created new gingerbreading from scratch to emulate the detailing under the balcony in the historic photo. Though most of the porch posts were rotten, he was able to save one to use and replicate to create the other posts. He also re-created the balcony balusters visible in the photo for use on the balcony as well as the porch, which hadn't existed at the time the photo was taken.

In the course of the renovation, Erin discovered, "I don't need a lot of stuff to make me happy." She and Rich have four children, most of whom have already left the nest, but love to visit the cottage. Even so, Erin remarks "When I'm there by myself, I don't feel overwhelmed; I feel like I fit."

Erin and Rich wanted the walls between bedrooms to extend to the ceiling, but they hated to lose daylight in the middle bedroom as a result. So they installed two leaded windows that they found at Nor'east Architectural Antiques in South Hampton, N.H., high in the wall to share daylight, add character, and maintain privacy.

# A SPEC WITH SIMPLICITY

ENGAGED WITH SITE

HUMAN SCALE

SIMPLE MASSING

SHELTERING ROOF

ECONOMY OF MEANS

INFORMALITY

SUNNY DISPOSITION

OPPOSITE COMPLEMENTS

CRAFTED DETAIL

Not stark modern . . . it's a lot richer.

**DESIGNED BY ARCHITECT JIM ESTES**, this long, skinny cottage in Jamestown, R.I., isn't your typical spec house. "The idea was to do something we normally wouldn't do. Usually spec houses are very safe—all decisions are made with the idea that the house will please a general audience. Not the case here," explains Jim. He wanted to have some fun with the design and make the most of the neighborhood site that's close to town but also within easy access of a deeded right-of-way to launch kayaks. The cottage's footprint maximizes the buildable area as determined by the town's required zoning setbacks. Because the side setbacks are equal, the house is in the middle of the lot, but it's oriented to engage with the landscape to the west, where the neighboring lot is open. The taller eastern facade, featuring smaller openings in a more solid wall, provides some privacy from the neighboring house.

The modest front north elevation features an attached storage shed with a sliding barn door that allows for a large, unencumbered opening. With the front door ajar, an arriving guest can catch a glimpse straight through the linear cottage and out to the rear yard.

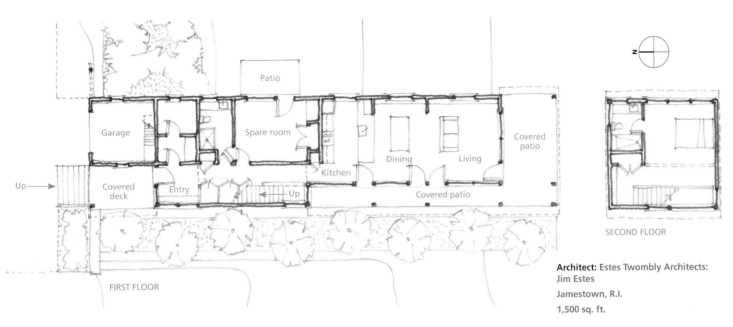

FIRST FLOOR

Patio

Garage

Spare room

Covered
patio

Covered
deck

Up

Entry

Kitchen

Dining

Living

Up

Covered patio

SECOND FLOOR

**Architect:** Estes Twombly Architects:
Jim Estes

Jamestown, R.I.

1,500 sq. ft.

Built into a plinth in the landscape, the long, simple shed forms extend deep into a
private rear yard and address the western side yard. The juxtaposition of the rough,
muted-gray, eastern white-pine siding and the sharp, striking, wrapping lines created
by its mitered installation is an interesting expression of opposite complements.

 The low, overhanging eaves (complete with rafter tails) protect the extensive western glazing from harsh afternoon daylight and reduce the scale of the building. The overhanging rake likewise protects the southern glazing. Exterior concrete pavers mesh well with the polished concrete floors of the interior, helping blend the outdoors with the indoors.

 The sunny entry hall with a gracious cathedral ceiling introduces visitors to the simple palette of warm maple veneer—here, in the form of a bench and closets—and darkly mottled, polished concrete floors. Together they set the stage for crisp informality.

Primarily one room wide and with the front and back doors aligned, Jim's design recalls the layout of the New Orleans Shotgun cottages, so named because a shot fired through the front door could exit clean through the building and out the opposite back door without hitting any intervening walls. A hallway next to the interior stair dissolves into an open kitchen, dining, and living area under a cathedral ceiling. The easily legible plan results in simple massing and draws those entering from the front porch stoop toward the more private back and western-facing yards. One of Jim's goals was to make the most of indoor/outdoor living in a fairly tight neighborhood while preserving privacy.

 Light floods into the kitchen from the western wall of nearly full-height glazing and doors. Stainless steel and honed limestone are introduced into the quiet palette. The IKEA dining table fits right in with the clean look.

 From the kitchen sink, the cook has commanding views to the south—through the dining and living areas—and west out the nearby wall of glazing. Daylight streams in from three directions. The board-finish cathedral ceiling adds texture and creates volume for the overlapping communal space that feels simultaneously cozy and airy.

 Maple veneer millwork built into the eastern wall of the informal common space helps define distinct zones: kitchen, dining, and living. Seeing all of the way through the house from the living area and out the front door lends clarity to the legible plan.

 Nearly floor to ceiling glass helps bring the western landscape into the living area and stretches the living area into the landscape, aided further by concrete underfoot inside and out. Colorful and patterned furnishings show well in the neutral setting.

Jim chose to use a shed roof for its simplicity. Plus, the low western eaves help shield the harsher daylight of late afternoons, while bringing the scale of the house down and providing comfortable shelter. Inside, a simple palette made up mostly of polished concrete floors, white wallboard, white trim, maple veneer, and a white cathedral board ceiling suggests an economy of means that's compatible with informal cottage living. Jim advises, "Keep it simple. I'm convinced it shows furniture and objects better." And spaces will flow together, so they feel larger. Honed limestone on the kitchen peninsula and hammered limestone on the bathroom floor provide refined accents that complement the more industrial aesthetic of the concrete floors and exterior concrete pavers.

A bank of nearly full-height glazing and glass doors on the western and southern walls of the multipurpose living space wash it with daylight and invite the outdoors in and indoors out. The stairway and bedroom loft also benefit from a run of glass above the stairs as well as a string of awning windows on the eastern wall of the bedroom. Sunny spaces, bright with daylight, can create warmth and coziness even in an open, contemporary space.

"It's not stark modern. We did a number of things to make it a lot richer," notes Jim. "We have all the rafter tails exposed on the eaves, which despite it being a more contemporary house, is a cottage sort of detail." The locally cut, rough 1×12 eastern white-pine siding with mitered corners also has a crafted cottage look. As does the living-space cathedral board ceiling notable for the ³/₃₂-in. groove Jim specified between boards, "which is like a lot of the old cottages you see with board interiors, after the boards have shrunk up over the years," he says.

So, no, this isn't your typical spec house. "The plan is pretty unusual. The siding is, too, as are the materials inside, like the concrete and the more contemporary detailing and cabinetwork," notes Jim. Well suited to a couple—young or old—or a single person attracted to its quiet simplicity and connection to the landscape, this spec house has more the feel of a custom, contemporary cottage.

The bedroom loft borrows daylight and view from the western windows in the stairwell. Because the bedroom is open to the stairs, it feels less contained and more generous.

Maple veneer plywood continues from the face of the under-stair cabinets up to form a simple, almost boat-like guardrail. Maple treads and a maple handrail echo the simple palette. The bottom landing extension signals a turn in the stairs and lends the closets scale.

# POCKET PATTERN

| ENGAGED WITH SITE | HUMAN SCALE | SIMPLE MASSING | SHELTERING ROOF | ECONOMY OF MEANS | INFORMALITY | SUNNY DISPOSITION | OPPOSITE COMPLEMENTS | CRAFTED DETAIL |

A pattern
with layers of
personal space.

IN SPRING VALLEY—a pocket neighborhood in Port Townsend, Wash.—
Sheri Price owns a cottage architect Ross Chapin calls the "Betty
Gable." It's a variation of a one-story, one-bedroom, side-gable cottage
he designed for Betty Lu, an 80-something-year-old in another pocket
neighborhood. The second iteration of the original "Betty Lu" cottage
was a two-bedroom version he named the "Betty Lu Lu." For the Port
Townsend pocket neighborhood, he rotated the cottage's gable, so it faces
front and dubbed it the Betty Gable.

 Sheri's Betty Gable cottage has five separate layers of personal space that transition from the sidewalk along the neighborhood green to the front door. The first is the 30-in.-wide swath of perennials that the developer planted; the second is the low fence; the third is the front garden; the fourth is the low porch guardrail, complete with flower boxes; the fifth is the porch itself.

The simple massing, sheltering gable and shed roofs, and the human-scaled porch and guardrail make for an inviting cottage. The unique painted panel of flowers that Ross created on the gable face amid the economical board-and-batten siding adds a custom, crafted touch.

**Architect: Ross Chapin Architects**
**Port Townsend, Wash.**
**838 sq. ft.**

"The front portion of this house, with the main room and the little alcove and the porch, is what really the 'Bettys' are about," explains Ross. In Spring Valley, he anchored the eastern edge of the nearly 1-acre 10-house pocket neighborhood with three Betty Gable cottages in a variety of compatible colors. They're further differentiated by the custom paintings he created for the face of the gable end of each. Front, side, and rear yard landscaping determined by the individual homeowners also makes each cottage distinct. A red, 2-story cottage that Ross calls the "Egret" acts as a landmark structure at the street end to the southwest. The three homes opposite the run of Betty Gable cottages are sibling "Betty Jane" 1-story, side-gable cottages. Two "Coho" cottages, which are 1½ stories, and a sweet little 1-story "Lisette" cottage round out the neighborhood of small dwellings. A modest side-gable commons building with a polycarbonate covered porch serves as a destination on the north end of the shared lawn. Together the cottages form a cohesive composition arranged around a commons, the hallmark of a pocket neighborhood.

Ross notes, "I approach designing a pocket neighborhood like a painter would a painting." So, among other

  Sheri's cozy porch looks across the green as do the other cottage porches in the pocket neighborhood. The small red cottage to the right is the common building at the head of the green, where the community gathers for potlucks, book groups, meetings, and the like.

things, he pays attention to creating a focal point, a calm center, a rich edge, secondary focal points, and transitions between spaces—like between the parking area and the central green. The structures, which are Ross's neighborhood building blocks, all display simple massing and sheltering roofs. In addition, they're punctuated with human-scaled front porches, which reinforce the neighborhood's sense of community.

When designing Spring Valley and the cottages within it, Ross applied a few particularly relevant patterns inspired by Christopher Alexander's master work *A Pattern Language*. One such pattern is "layers of personal space." Ross created five layers of space that transition in stages from the public sidewalk in front of Sheri's cottage to the semi-public in-between zones and ultimately to the private entry door, all of which help engage the cottage with the site. "With these, a stranger will feel the boundaries of private territory, an invited guest will feel a special sense of arrival, and a resident will feel the comfort of home and the pleasure of community," he explains.

Inside Sheri's cottage, personal space is similarly layered, from the informal open living and kitchen area facing the community commons to the slightly more private intimacy

 A long flowerbox provides another opportunity to layer space and add a personal touch to the cottage. Sheri says that often when she comes home at the end of the day, she likes to putter around the house while the top portion of the Dutch door is open, inviting breezes and connection with neighbors passing by.

of the dining nook, on to the more private back hall and bedrooms, and ultimately out to the private rear yard.

The concept of a layered treatment also applies to layers of crafted detail which, when part of a larger whole, helps enrich the character of the cottage. The economical, mostly Sheetrock interior walls and ceilings gain depth with the application of considered trim. On the tall, flat ceiling, simple, applied ½-in. by 2-in. battens over the Sheetrock add pattern and dimension. Where the ceiling meets the wall, a pared-down crown of sorts, composed of two trim boards, finesse

the transition. A third, lower trim board wraps the wall of the open space at the height of the built-in bookcase top rail, the window trim, and the openings into the nook and work-counter recess, softening the scale of the tall wall and helping unify and organize the spaces into a larger room rather than disparate smaller zones.

Sheri's favorite spot in the cottage is the dining nook. It's a sunny, human-scaled getaway off the more open, taller volume of the kitchen/living area. Almost boat-like in how it's fitted to folks sharing a meal, the nook nicely complements

 The cottage massing steps down toward the back—a form of three-dimensional layering—and terminates with a small bracketed rooflet over glass sliders leading from the bedroom to the private rear yard. Though the materials are basic and affordable, the assembled craftsmanship adds richness and depth.

 Ross believes color is an important component of design. When the late afternoon sun strikes the melon-colored rake frieze boards, they glow, appearing to lift the roof. The three stacked trim boards that define the rake of the three stepped roofs are another example of layered detail that enlivens and completes the look.

The dining nook includes a lowered, 1×6 pine, tongue-and-groove ceiling for additional warmth. The wraparound windows give the nook a porch-like feel. The maple butcher-block table is a purposeful and readily available stock material that matches the kitchen island countertop.

 A propane stove serves as the hearth of the home. Recessing it within a crafted centerpiece, flanked by built-in bookcases, dresses up the living area. The 10-ft.-tall, board-and-batten ceiling and layered crown and wall trim add cottage character with lofty reach.

# POCKET NEIGHBORHOODS

A pocket is a protected space where we tuck special things for safe keeping beyond the fray. The small, cluster communities within larger communities that Ross Chapin began shaping in 1996—composed of no more than a dozen compact homes arranged around a common space in which the neighbors all have a stake—struck him as pockets of sorts too. He began referring to them as *pocket neighborhoods* and the name took hold.

"The prevailing opportunity in America is to live on your own lot or in an apartment (where you've got no say). This is in between. This is saying, the people who live here want to be in a neighborly setting. That comes with a certain responsibility," explains Ross. He believes in limiting the number of homes in a pocket neighborhood to what he describes as the "scale of

sociability," while also preserving personal privacy. He compares it to thinking about the size of a group of people around a dinner table who together comfortably engage in a lively discussion. Such diners, like those who live in a pocket neighborhood, feel connected to each other and enjoy being part of a community. Pocket neighborhoods are suited to single people, both younger and older, couples, families of one or two parents with children, adult children with aging parents—really, all kinds of households.

A common building for gatherings usually sits at the head of the shared open space, which may be a garden, a lawn, a pedestrian street, a courtyard, or some other mutually beneficial outdoor environment. Pocket neighborhoods differ from co-housing in that in a pocket neighborhood a sense

of community may arise naturally or organically due to residents living closely around a shared commons, whereas in co-housing the community is intentionally formed by people with shared values and goals who may even participate in the building of the community itself. "This is kind of in between co-housing and a traditional development," Ross clarifies.

For Sheri, the Spring Valley pocket neighborhood has been a comfortable fit because, as she says with a laugh, her teenage daughter has four sets of supplementary grandparents there. To learn more about pocket neighborhoods and the design principles that shape them, refer to Ross's book *Pocket Neighborhoods: Creating Small-Scale Community in a Large-Scale World*.

the greater volume of the space it abuts. It also lends daylight to the adjacent space, which has smaller, higher windows on both ends, so Sheri isn't peering into her neighbors' homes. This attention to preserving privacy from cottage to cottage is the foundation of the pattern Ross refers to as "nested houses," which suggests that cottages with one side that's more open and one side that's more closed nest well together, making for a neighborly arrangement.

Ross summarizes that Sheri's Betty Gable in her pocket neighborhood is a cottage for townsfolk today. "It's an every-person's house," he says. Sheri adds, "Having a smaller footprint on the world was appealing too."

 The smaller dining nook complements the greater volume of the kitchen it abuts. Each borrows visually from the other, lending the kitchen greater intimacy and the nook some expansiveness.

 Scrolled sides on modest glass overhead cabinets add welcome detail to the open kitchen. PaperStone® counters, factory seconds, add richness while maintaining the budget. The tall ceiling lends the kitchen an unexpected spaciousness.

# FAMILY CAMP

ENGAGED WITH SITE · HUMAN SCALE · SIMPLE MASSING · SHELTERING ROOF · ECONOMY OF MEANS · INFORMALITY · SUNNY DISPOSITION · OPPOSITE COMPLEMENTS · WABI SABI · CRAFTED DETAIL

It's simple living.

THE COTTAGE IN JANE TREACY'S FAMILY is part of a former Methodist campground on Cape Cod in Massachusetts. Like the Martha's Vineyard campground (see p. 155), the Cape campground dates back to the mid-1800s and is made up of small cottages that stand on the footprints of former tents that were sprinkled around grounds, which included a tabernacle. The Cape campground contains roughly 60 acres and only about 70 cottages, so structures are spaced farther apart in a wooded setting; its tabernacle is no longer standing, having been damaged in the hurricanes of 1938 and 1944. Thankfully, much of the tabernacle's contents, like chairs and china, survive in the collections of current cottage owners.

Nestled in a small clearing, the original cottage sits to the left and the porch and second-story addition sit to the right. The simple, modest massing maintains the cottage's human scale. The two gabled forms—one smaller and one larger—also make for a composition of opposite complements.

"One of the most used rooms is the screen porch," notes Jane. It further engages the cottage with the site. The porch swing came from a yard sale. A neighboring cottage can be glimpsed beyond, not too close yet not too far away, maintaining privacy while creating a sense of community.

The addition built behind the original c. 1880 cottage matches the original's steep 14/12 Gothic Revival style, pitched, sheltering roof. Affordable Texture 1-11 (T1-11) siding on the addition plays off the vertical-board siding on the front of the original. Jane says the T1-11 could receive another finish, like shingles, should they decide to insulate someday.

The whitewashed open stud interior speaks to informal seasonal cottage living. Leaving the ceiling framing and structural decking above unfinished adds a warm contrast and boat-like feel. The addition sits a couple of steps below the original cottage to gain first-floor headroom.

The intimate scale of the original cottage makes it the perfect spot for quiet reading time in the evenings. Tall front windows and the open front door welcome abundant daylight that feels all the sunnier thanks to the colorful furnishings. The rocker and the Morris chair (cropped in the foreground) came with the cottage.

 Pot hooks and open shelves across the open studs add playful touches to the cottage's hardworking galley kitchen. The sink came with the cottage. Jane opted not to include a dishwasher, noting "hand washing dishes is part of cottage life."

**Homeowner architect:**
Treacy & Eagleburger Architects PC

Cape Cod, Mass.

± 700 sq. ft. +
120-sq.-ft. screen porch

Since the Cape campground is a cooperative in which cottage purchasers own a share of the campground land, the cottages are not generally listed conventionally with a multiple listing service. Jane's mom, Elizabeth, a schoolteacher who summered on the Cape, was lucky enough to hear through the grapevine that one was for sale. When Elizabeth acquired it with Jane and her three sisters, Cynthia, Suzanne, and Lisa, the seasonal cottage was two rooms deep. The original front cottage was a 10-ft. by 12-ft. living area with a sleeping loft within a steep Gothic Revival gable roof. The back room was a 10-ft. by 10-ft. kitchen addition with a low-pitched roof. A water closet, accessed from outside, was the caboose to the kitchen.

Once the cottage was theirs, the family cleaned it up, salvaged items the previous owners left behind, and used the cottage for several summers as it was. Then Jane, an architect—with her husband, Phil Eagleburger, also an architect acting as design critic—proposed an addition that the family agreed would significantly improve it. "We felt very strongly

Just steps from the kitchen, the table and chairs that came with the cottage are surrounded by wall openings on three sides—one window that captures eastern light, two windows that look into the screen porch to the south, and a north-facing French door—creating an inviting spot for a variety of activities. Many of the flea market and antique treasures that Jane and her family have collected over the years find a home in the nearby shelves.

  Jane created an alcove off the master bedroom addition to accommodate a loveseat for visitors with a small child or for a guest who might want to tuck away to read. The steeply pitched roof of the addition provides sheltering cover and more headroom than the original front roof.

that the addition should have the same roof pitch and to carry the spirit of the original cottage," explains Jane. The family decided to abandon the old back kitchen addition and attached water closet. Instead, Jane proposed the two-story add-on that steps back from the original cottage rather than builds on top of it. The addition includes a south-facing screen porch with a new master bedroom above, featuring a cross-gable dormer. A north-facing, cross-gable extension houses the kitchen on the first floor and a full bath above, smartly stacking the plumbing. Shifting the mass of the addition to the south meant Jane could locate a new stair beneath the peak of the taller addition. "That whole stepping routine keeps the scale very comfortable," notes Jane. It also creates an interesting exterior dynamic where the front, little gable structure complements the back, larger gable structure. Before

they built the addition, they first constructed a full basement 40 ft. to the south and moved the original cottage on top.

The addition has exposed framing just as the original cottage does, which helps the two blend together and reinforces the informality of summer cottage living. Floors on the main level and the second-level addition are simple, painted plywood. The floor above the original living area is structural decking since Jane didn't want to add any additional floor joists there. The 1950s-era kitchen base cabinets were recycled from one of Jane and Phil's projects. They added beadboard to the back so the cabinets fit right in. The front stoop balustrades were Suzanne's find from Takoma Park, Md. "My whole family likes to go to antiques shops, antiques auctions," says Jane. Their unique finds are on display throughout the cottage.

When Jane and her family are enjoying the cottage, they spend their time whiling away the better part of the day out on the screen porch, tending to the heather garden that Elizabeth created, playing games and assembling puzzles at the kitchen table as well as reading in the evenings in the front living area. There's talk about creating another small addition to contain another bedroom, bathroom, and maybe a sleeping loft since the family's next generation is expanding. They might insulate a future addition, so there would be a place to stay in the chillier shoulder seasons. But the family is hesitant to insulate the rest of the cottage because that would alter its character, and they wouldn't want to change what they love about the cottage. "It's the simplicity of it, you know; there isn't that much to worry about when you're there. It's simple living," muses Jane.

A playful barn slider serves the master bedroom and adds crafted character and color to the stair hall. A friend found the old sign and knew it would be perfect for the cottage.

The front twin bedroom under the original cottage's steep roof is a cozy cottage hideaway. The tall original front window has a big impact on the small space, helping it feel more expansive. Corks receive nail tips and act a bit like bumpers.

# ISLAND FOLK

ENGAGED WITH SITE    HUMAN SCALE    SIMPLE MASSING    SHELTERING ROOF    ECONOMY OF MEANS    INFORMALITY    SUNNY DISPOSITION    OPPOSITE COMPLEMENTS    WABI SABI    CRAFTED DETAIL

> A balance of defined spaces on the interior . . . and moments that focus on the exterior.

EMILY AND CLAY RIVES'S C. 1890 COTTAGE on Martha's Vineyard reminds me of my mother-in-law's place on the island and the Vineyard vernacular in general. You might call these dwellings folk cottages or agrarian cottages. They're generally 1½-story, human-scaled, gabled forms, often with a front porch, arranged with simple massing, sometimes in an ell or, as Emily and Clay's cottage does, stepping back into a lot that is considerably deeper than it is wide. And like many of the island cottages, Emily's has been in her family for years. It was her childhood home for a time when it was a two-family house (despite its small size). Recently, not long before beginning a family of their own, she and Clay decided to turn it into a single-family cottage to enjoy as a getaway.

The front gable end of the human-scaled folk cottage with simple massing typifies the Vineyard vernacular. Clad Marvin double-hung windows with two lites over two lites match the window style of those they replaced. The original stone front stoop was left intact.

The new porch off the kitchen adds 150 sq. ft. of informal outdoor living space to complement the enclosed kitchen, nearly doubling its size. Only three steps above grade, the back porch provides comfortable access to the landscape it engages. New gable dormers in the sheltering roof are partially visible through the tree leaves.

When fully open, the Marvin folding door helps further unite the kitchen and outdoor living space, which are at the same level. A horizontal retractable Centor screen system can be deployed when bugs are an issue. New white-cedar shingles clad the exterior of the cottage, and shiplap—used in places throughout the cottage— makes an appearance on the porch ceiling.

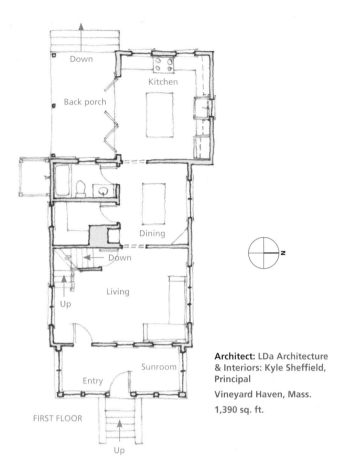

Down

Kitchen

Back porch

Dining

Down

Living

Up

Entry

Sunroom

Up

FIRST FLOOR

**Architect:** LDa Architecture & Interiors: Kyle Sheffield, Principal

Vineyard Haven, Mass.

**1,390 sq. ft.**

The outdoor shower backs up to the bathroom and is defined by the same red-cedar posts as the porch. Here, the crafted shiplap is red cedar too. All of the cedar will weather gray to relate to the natural environment. A full-height barn slider (composed of the same cedar) provides privacy and stores neatly away thanks to a slot carved in the deck.

One afternoon, they drove their architect friend Kyle Sheffield, a principal at LDa Architecture & Interiors, by the cottage and later found themselves sketching design ideas in the sand at the beach. Kyle and Clay had met singing a cappella in college and were both alumni of Vineyard Sound, an island summer a cappella group. Kyle was familiar with the island vernacular since he had grown up summering there and later taught sailing there too. Soon the three were collaborating in earnest on renovation plans for the cottage. It wasn't long before what started as a kitchen and two-bathroom remodel morphed into a whole-cottage renovation.

Even though the structure was taken down to the studs and sheathing, the cottage had tremendous sentimental value to Emily, and it was important to her that the renovation look back as it looked forward. One way the new design reflects Emily's memory of the cottage is that the first-floor general room locations and uses and much of the second-floor room locations and uses remain as they were.

Entry is still through the enclosed front porch, into the living area, back to the dining area, and into the rear kitchen. What's changed on the first floor, beyond finishes and exterior windows, is the definition of those spaces—in plan and ceiling configuration—and the resulting improved, informal

    Emily chose the Blissful Blue (Sherwin-Williams) paint color for the floor of the enclosed porch to evoke the memory of the space when it was her childhood room. The wall and sheltering ceiling finish introduces those entering the cottage to the shiplap that weaves in and out of the interior.

 Like the rest of the first-floor common spaces, the living room features refinished, original heart-pine floors, which exude a warm, lived-in character. The windows between the living room and enclosed porch are the originals, newly refurbished, which also honor the cottage's history. Emily chose neutral furnishings so as not to compete with the architecture. "The house really is the main event," she says.

# A GREAT ROOM FOR TODAY

Many of the cottages in these pages contain what might be called a "great room." But these are not the great rooms of McMansions or ill-conceived developments. The term may have come into vogue in the go-go 1990s to describe a large, open shared living/dining/kitchen area. But such great rooms were generally overscaled spaces that were completely open or almost completely open beneath uncomfortably tall, flat or vaulted ceilings with little or no differentiation between spaces other than perhaps a change of flooring material in the kitchen. A cottage in and around that era or earlier wouldn't generally have contained a great room by virtue of a cottage's small scale and typical collection of smaller rooms.

But, in today's cottages, what makes a great room great is that it welcomes the benefits of a shared common, more public living/dining/kitchen space in a smaller dwelling while recognizing the need to provide architectural definition to the different uses within that space. Such definition can contribute to scale and comfort, while signaling a change of activity. In many cases, subtle differentiation can even help a small cottage live larger. In renovations, such as Emily and Clay Rives's cottage, aligning and widening openings between the common spaces and beyond can help the spaces overlap while remaining somewhat distinct. In new, more open construction, ceiling treatment—in the form of collar ties or a change in plane and/or material or the introduction of beams—can provide a visual cue as to spatial scale and change of use. Other interventions like posts, half walls, interior transoms, or even floor-plane changes can communicate nuanced spatial demarcation. A successful twenty-first-century cottage gives a great room new definition, paying attention to comfort and scale.

flow and access to the outdoors and outdoor living. Kyle slightly rearranged the first floor to resolve an awkward entrance to the basement stairs, shifted some space from the dining area to the living area by removing a closet and chimney, and reoriented the kitchen to connect to a new back porch that better engages the site and the outdoors.

In the process, he relocated and slightly widened the interior doorways between the spaces so they align and enable visual connection through the living areas and out a rear kitchen window, which entices those entering to circulate through what seems like a larger home than it actually is. "We really did stay true to some of the original room footprints but opened it up in unexpected ways," says Emily. Kyle was careful to keep some differentiation between the spaces while better integrating them. "It's a great room without being a great room," Emily continues. Kyle also converted the cavernous, first-floor full bathroom into a dramatically more efficient full bath and an adjacent, compact home office for Clay.

The new back porch maximizes the limited room for expansion on the property. "The only area that we could capture was in the knuckle of the ell off the back of the house,"

The dining room also features the refinished heart-pine floors and painted-white surfaces found elsewhere in the house as well as a recurring blue accent. Here, the blue is on the inside of the back of the original corner hutch.

Raising the ceiling in the kitchen to the roughly 9-ft. height of the collar ties of the sheltering roof helps the kitchen feel larger than its footprint. As with the porches, shiplap can be found on the ceiling; it's also a backdrop for a custom pot rack. The rosewood butcher-block top on the blue island will develop a rich patina over time.

Kyle says. So he conceived of the new porch off the kitchen to create a transitional, informal, outdoor living space between the indoors and the open space of the backyard, where Emily and Clay like to grill. Opening the kitchen to the porch, which is at the same level as the kitchen, via a generous four-panel Marvin folding door brings the outdoors in and the indoors out, brightening the kitchen and lending it spaciousness. The same width as the kitchen but open on two sides, Kyle's porch design complements the kitchen it flanks. "He added a room without actually adding a room," notes Emily.

On the second floor, Kyle made similarly discreet floor plan changes, shaping more functional closets for the two existing front bedrooms and converting what had been an apartment kitchen into the master bedroom, which also benefits from some additional space acquired from the reconfigured bathroom. Originally, the rooms beneath the sheltering roof had limited headroom and contained only one window each on the gable ends, so access to daylight and ventilation was minimal. While acknowledging the coziness of the sheltering roof, Kyle understood that adding dormers would make the upstairs more comfortable. Four new gable dormers improve head height, daylighting, and cross ventilation.

Kyle and the couple's choice of a succinct finish palette contributes a fresh updated look while also helping the cottage feel more sizable. Nearly every surface is painted the same white in different sheens, with some notable blue exceptions. The economy of means includes crafted shiplap, which makes an appearance in many different applications throughout the house. "The idea of this shiplap started to become a stitch from room to room," says Kyle. "The key was, in my mind, not to make it a one-trick pony and use it everywhere so it starts to lose its luster," he explains. Shiplap can be found

 The shiplap (with a ¼-in. reveal) creates a custom crafted look in the stair hall, which also displays original southern yellow-pine treads. A new Marvin oval window adds a port-hole like whimsical touch. It's trimmed with 1-in.-square stock, which is used on the jambs of the openings in the shiplap throughout.

on the walls and sheltering ceiling of the front porch, wrapping the stair walls, on the ceilings of the kitchen and back porch, in areas of the bathrooms, and as a backdrop for a custom pot rack.

Since completing the cottage renovation, Emily and Clay have welcomed their son, John Lloyd, into the family. Now that she has a crawler, Emily appreciates the new sightlines through the cottage even more. "It's cozy but airy at the same time. We're on top of each other, but there's enough space and sense of place for each unique area of the house," she notes. Soon they'll be turning their focus to further augmenting the landscape they view from the enclosed front porch and from the kitchen and its open porch. "I would say that a cottage for today is a balance of defined spaces on the interior but also moments that really focus on the exterior," Kyle notes. Emily and Clay's cottage fits the bill.

 The master bathroom enjoys greater headroom and daylight thanks to the new two-window dormer within the sheltering roof. Shiplap behind the vanity mirrors provides an accent rather than a full-room treatment. The custom Douglas fir vanity by Crown Point Cabinetry is topped with Carrara marble, in keeping with the neutral color theme. The floor is porcelain-ceramic tile that resembles driftwood.

# MARLBORO MUSIC COTTAGES

| ENGAGED WITH SITE | HUMAN SCALE | SIMPLE MASSING | SHELTERING ROOF | ECONOMY OF MEANS | INFORMALITY | SUNNY DISPOSITION | OPPOSITE COMPLEMENTS | WABI SABI | CRAFTED DETAIL |

A satisfying mix
of the familiar and
the unexpected.

**BEFORE VISITING THE MARLBORO MUSIC FESTIVAL** on the grounds of Marlboro College in Vermont, architects Joan Soranno and John Cook of HGA in Minnesota had an altogether different idea of the retreat dwellings they might design for the summer festival. Known for their modern sensibility, the HGA architects had visions of very contemporary structures befitting the worldly classical musicians who attend the festival. Once on location, when they saw the leisurely arranged mostly white-clapboard farm buildings that make up the campus and learned about the informal, communal, egalitarian culture of the festival, they adjusted their thinking. They realized their design would need to be grounded in the tradition of New England building

With their simple massing, the Cape Cod cottage–inspired retreats nestle in clearings among trees and within view of old fieldstone walls. The pared-down forms (like this Cottage #3) include sheltering roofs and low, human-scaled eaves.

A limited exterior palette of red cedar shiplap siding, Vermont slate roofs, split-face stone foundations, and zinc elements relate the cottages to the site's context, coloring, and evolving changes. Zinc knife-edge eaves and thin rake detailing on the sheltering roof contribute a crisp, current look. "We were trying to put a contemporary spin on these," notes Joan.

and the context of the Green Mountains, while looking ahead to the festival's innovative future. They found inspiration on the campus itself, in the Cape buildings in their midst. Joan studied the 400-year-old Cape Cod cottage typology in order to understand its essence and to determine how the architects might best reinterpret it to suit Marlboro Music's housing needs today.

Those needs involved accommodating some of the invited senior artists and their families in new residences near campus. To that end, Marlboro Music acquired, with the aid of a generous donor, 15 acres from Marlboro College on which to construct five retreat dwellings adjacent to the campus. The balance of the senior artists live in on- and off-campus apartments, and the young professional musicians

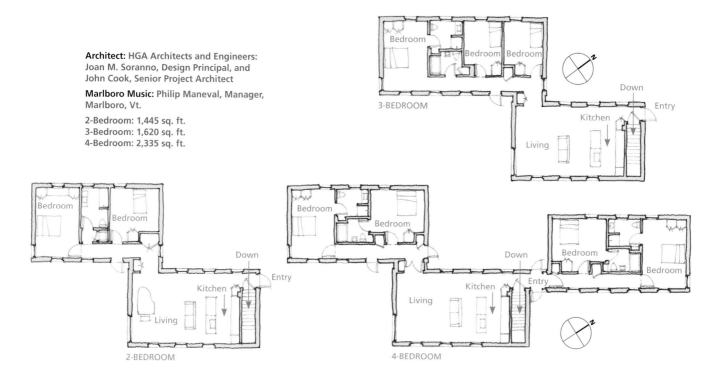

**Architect:** HGA Architects and Engineers: Joan M. Soranno, Design Principal, and John Cook, Senior Project Architect

**Marlboro Music:** Philip Maneval, Manager, Marlboro, Vt.

2-Bedroom: 1,445 sq. ft.
3-Bedroom: 1,620 sq. ft.
4-Bedroom: 2,335 sq. ft.

live in the Marlboro College dormitories. Marlboro Music Manager Philip Maneval penned a short brief describing the festival's architectural goals, which included creating three two-bedroom residences, one three-bedroom residence, and one four-bedroom residence to be occupied by potentially two families or four unrelated senior artists. Because it was important to Marlboro Music to maintain a sense of parity among all of the musicians, the new retreats would need to be simple and somewhat modest so as not to render the existing accommodations wanting.

After walking the undeveloped wooded site accessed by an abandoned logging road, the architects determined that the least invasive approach would be to site the new residences off the existing road, now known as Musician's Way. They identified five locations in which the dwellings could engage with relatively flat grade, aligned with the property's natural contours so as not to disturb it. Each site has access to daylight and at least partial views of the property's 150-year-old stone walls, as well as the potential for privacy between the dwellings.

The site-specific, Cape-inspired cottages that the architects designed are composed of two or three staggered, gabled components connected at the corners and featuring parallel ridges in alignment with adjacent contours. The simple massing is divided into public and private areas such that one gabled component houses the public kitchen/dining/living space and another gabled component (or two) houses the private bedroom/bathroom spaces. Entry is generally from the short end of the public component. A circulation path along the edge doesn't interfere with use of the public area and jogs along the closest edge of the private component, making room for the bedrooms and bathrooms.

Each gabled component is defined by a low, human-scaled, 7-ft. roof spring line based on the traditionally low eaves of the Cape Cod cottage precedent. "We wanted these to be really intimate in their relationship to the surrounding landscape," notes Joan. But unlike historic Capes, which paired low ceilings with low eaves, the ceilings of the public spaces and the master bedrooms in the retreats benefit from cathedral ceilings beneath the steeply sheltering roofs. Joan had determined in her evaluation of the Cape Cod cottage precedent that walls typically contributed to 40% of a Cape's height and that the roof contributed the remaining 60%. This emphasis on the roof was primarily in response to the New England climate and potential for harsh weather. At Marlboro Music, the architects opted to exaggerate the proportion some. "It looks a little more top heavy. And to us, it was just a little bit more beautiful," says Joan.

As an alternative to the white clapboards found elsewhere on the Marlboro College campus, which visually pop, Joan and John chose to side the cottage retreats with durable red cedar shiplap treated with a weathering stain, which will gray over time and blend in further with the woodlands. The cleanly crafted zinc window and door jambs, eaves, and rake

Clear-finished, flush, indigenous white pine walls beneath sheltering, rhythmic pine rafters and pine decking in the common living area establish a quiet backdrop to sizable views of the lush landscape. The low, 7-ft., human-scaled roof spring line above the Vermont slate floor creates intimate edges that soar to a central ridge. Joan adds, "The acoustical performance of this shape works really well."

trim as well as the zinc-clad chimneys (which consolidate all the building's venting) will continue to oxidize gray. Joan adds, "We didn't want the architecture to shout, because you've got this beautiful scenery around you with these beautiful trees."

Inside, clear-finished, local white pine abounds. It's used on the walls—complete with crafted flush window and door casings—and for the structural decking of the ceilings, which is further defined by timber rafters receiving the structural insulated panels (SIPs) of the roof. The pine lends the cottages a warm, informal aesthetic. Floors are Vermont slate, which is well suited to radiant heat and, it turns out, also benefits the acoustics. The architects deliberately chose a limited palette to reflect an economy of means. "That kind of monochrome sometimes is very calming," says Joan.

Large windows are another departure from the traditional Cape. Operable floor-to-ceiling Marvin casement windows provide ventilation and ample daylight as well as an opportunity to connect with views of the rock walls, trees, and nearby wetlands. They're also placed, in part, to limit views of neighboring cottages, while inviting the outdoors in and indoors out. Small high windows in the cathedral spaces offer some glimpses of treetops, and from the exterior, suggest the small windows often found in a Cape's attic story.

Animated over seven summer weeks by the comings and goings of senior artists and their families as well as the occasional sound of practicing within, these cottage retreats have become an integral part of Marlboro Music. (When not in use by the festival, the cottages are often leased to Marlboro College for faculty or student housing.) Settling into the treescape adjacent to the campus, they've proven a satisfying mix of the familiar and the unexpected. They're cottage retreats for the twenty-first century.

The master bedroom enjoys a cathedral sheltering ceiling, which lends it a bit of unexpected grandeur. The other bedrooms have flat, beamed, more typically intimate ceilings. The finishes in all of the bedrooms are the same as the shared kitchen/dining/living area.

## MARLBORO MUSIC FESTIVAL

Founded in 1951 by pianist Rudolf Serkin as well as Adolf and Hermann Busch and Marcel, Blanche, and Louis Moyse, Marlboro Music gathers approximately 85 professional musicians from around the world to their annual seven-week advanced-study center. "It's almost like a commune of exceptional musicians," says Philip Maneval, the manager of Marlboro Music. Each summer, about 60 young professional musicians,

selected via a competitive audition process, join about 25 invited senior artists who are acclaimed chamber musicians and recitalists and sometimes principal chairmembers of orchestras to collaborate, rehearse, and live side by side in a rural, retreat setting.

"We are really the original music festival in the United States, and the place, I feel, where chamber music was really born in the United States," says Philip.

During the latter half of the festival, performances, which are not predetermined, are an outgrowth of intensive rehearsal and collaboration during the first half. "It's an incredible combination of fun-loving, supportive, nurturing, family environment with an incredibly high artistic standard," concludes Philip. You might say the same of the retreat cottages themselves.

Open kitchens also constructed of pine and Vermont slate include a modest dining area built into a simple kitchen island. Circulation along the edge and under a low, compressed ceiling beyond, ending in a window view, contrasts the release of the common area's cathedral ceiling.

# MINI SALT BOX

ENGAGED WITH SITE

HUMAN SCALE

SIMPLE MASSING

SHELTERING ROOF

ECONOMY OF MEANS

INFORMALITY

SUNNY DISPOSITION

OPPOSITE COMPLEMENTS

WABI SABI

CRAFTED DETAIL

THE "SALT BOX," AS IT'S KNOWN ON HARBOUR ISLAND in the Bahamas, dates back to 1800 and had fallen into a state of disrepair when designer Tom Sheerer acquired, restored, and gently updated it, keeping its historic character in mind. William and Laura Young then came along and fell in love with it. "It's literally our idea of heaven," says William. They purchased it from Tom Sheerer and acquired an adjacent piece of property as well.

*A cottage retreat for today's informal indoor/outdoor living.*

 The Mini Salt Box cottage retreat sits at the eastern end of the pool, helping shape an outdoor room around it. The original Salt Box (not shown) edges the south side of the pool.

Taking inspiration from the simple massing of the original Salt Box, its hardy materials, and similar palette, this cottage retreat has mini-me appeal, thanks in part to the its human scale.

**Architectural designer:**
FGS Design LLC: Kiko Sanchez
**Interiors:** Lindroth Design: Amanda Lindroth and Celine Lotmore
Harbour Island, The Bahamas
436 sq. ft.

Next, they turned to architectural designer Kiko Sanchez, who worked with a local architect of record, to address their design goals. They wanted to supplement the three-bedroom Salt Box—located inland in town—with a pool, a pool house/guesthouse, and a dining porch. Kiko suggested combining the proposed uses into a single building oriented toward the pool. It was Laura who suggested where to place the new structure to help the three components of main house, pool, and pool house/guesthouse work together to engage the site with the existing gardens and the fruit trees they expected to plant.

Taking inspiration from the original Salt Box, the Mini Salt Box (as they call it) resembles the simple massing of the main house's gabled form within parapet end walls; its human-scaled, lean-to porch; and sympathetic building materials. The exterior walls of the Salt Box are made of coral stone quarried from its basement during excavation. The exterior walls of the Mini Salt Box cottage retreat are a similar color, but rendered in stucco, and feature crafted paneled shutters made out of sapele like the main house.

The layout of the Mini Salt Box includes a center bathroom flanked on either side by a guest bedroom, each with direct access to the bathroom and the west-facing front porch. The only shower for the building is an informal outdoor shower that can be accessed from both the outside and within the bathroom. The tight louvers of the full-height shutters offer enough privacy for the shower to function independently from the rest of the bathroom or as part of it. The porch fronts the cottage at the end of the pool. It includes a dining table and kitchenette on one end and a sitting area on the other. "We thought it would be fun to have indoor/outdoor dining there," says Laura. The louvered shutters can be closed to ward off rain or filter western light while still welcoming breezes.

Inside, William and Laura looked again to the Salt Box for finish inspiration. White painted shiplap boards—like those at the main house—line the entryway walls and sheltering tray ceilings in the bedrooms and bathroom, providing a consistent economy of means. The tiles on the entryway and bathroom floors are encaustic cement tiles, known as Cuban tiles locally. There are Cuban tiles in the main house kitchen, but they're a more traditional pattern. Lindroth Design helped guide finish selections like the tile shape and color choice at the cottage retreat. "I'm a sucker for anything blue," notes Laura.

"When everything is open and you're looking through the house, I really wanted a statement. I wanted to see that beautiful claw-foot tub. I wanted to see a really stunning, fun tile. And as you look onward, you have the outdoor shower," explains Laura. Team that with the indoor/outdoor dining area provided by the porch, and you have a cottage retreat for today's informal indoor/outdoor living. "The feel is very relaxed, a bit rough around the edges," summarizes William.

The sunny and airy guest bedroom features a sheltering tray ceiling with the same painted board finish as the end wall that borders the entry. The scale of the narrow double doors lends the modestly sized space a more gracious and generous feel.

Dutch-style shutters on the doors from one of the guest bedrooms open onto the informal indoor/outdoor dining area. The kitchenette features a hidden undercounter refrigerator (to the left) and open shelves that provide easy access to tableware. A custom, crisp parson's table contrasts the rugged coralina stone porch floor that resembles floors of the same material as the original Salt Box.

   The focal point of the interior—the bathroom's claw-foot tub—sits on a sunny blue encaustic cement tile, known as Cuban tile. The narrow French doors open onto the outdoor shower. Brass finishes throughout, like those in the original Salt Box, will darken with age, adding character.

# BACKYARD STUDIO

ENGAGED WITH SITE    HUMAN SCALE    SIMPLE MASSING    SHELTERING ROOF    ECONOMY OF MEANS    INFORMALITY    SUNNY DISPOSITION    OPPOSITE COMPLEMENTS    CRAFTED DETAIL

A grown-up play space to make art and music.

**WE HAD A PLAYHOUSE IN THE BACKYARD** when I was growing up. It was an old corn crib that my folks cleaned up and whitewashed. It was heaven. Ever since, I've been captivated by the idea of a small play space out back, so I'm a little envious of the owners of this studio who are lucky enough to have a grown-up play space to make art and music in their backyard in Jamestown, R.I.

 Amid the informal board-and-batten siding, the south elevation gable end features an approximately 10-ft.-tall by 4-ft.-wide single-hung window in the common space. Compare the size of it to that of the French entry doors to get a sense of the game it's playing with scale.

The sheltering shed roof of the art studio is sloped down to the south to reduce its visual scale from the street, while the roof's high side faces north to capture diffuse light. Approximately door-sized corner windows animate the elevation and the art studio.

**Architect:** Estes Twombly Architects: Peter Twombly

Jamestown, R.I.

820 sq. ft.

Peter Twombly of Estes Twombly collaborated with them to design the multipurpose ell-shaped cottage retreat, which sits in the northeast corner of their property diagonally across from their cross-gabled, turn-of-the-century main house. The studio's location helps close off a corner of the property, providing privacy and engaging the site by shaping a large yard in between it and the main house, which is pushed close to the opposite lot lines. While the color of the clapboards on the main house inspired the studio's exterior color and the steep roof pitch of the main house gable informed the steep pitch of the studio's gable, the two buildings are otherwise distinct. "Neither one of us is wedded to the idea that everything has to look like an old building, but a new version. So we liked the idea of having it incorporate modern elements but some classic architectural themes. It accomplishes both," explains the wife.

The studio's simple massing is composed of a 1-story, shed-roofed form that contains the wife's art studio and a 1½-story gabled form that houses the husband's recording studio as well as the family's bonus gathering room and loft where their two daughters hang out with friends. A flat-roofed entry and full bathroom occupy the space between the two studio wings. The three distinct volumes provide spatial variety and complement each other. "It's the quintessential house form in a way, with the chimney coming up the side," notes Peter.

Clad in eastern pine board-and-batten siding and featuring sheltering simple overhanging eaves and rake details, the studio retreat looks the part of a modest, informal cottage outbuilding. Oversized windows further reduce the scale of the already small retreat. What's more, the generous windows admit abundant daylight through fewer openings than if there had been more numerous conventionally sized windows, which was also a cost-saving decision for the budget-conscious project. Further, you could argue that the oversized windows, which are the opposite in scale of the walls they inhabit, complement the modest walls, resulting in a cute cottage facade.

A crisp interior of white walls and trim contrasts a serviceable concrete slab floor in the art studio and a warm, stained poplar floor in the recording studio and bonus hang-out space. White rod ties in the airy cathedral bonus space fit right in with the spare palette. The wife notes, "I think it has a really nice contemporary feel, but at the same time it doesn't feel super modern or cold at all." Peter concludes, "It's a pretty simple little structure."

The bonus hang-out space is washed with daylight from the oversized windows, while a woodstove offers a cozy cottage touch. The husband (who's a lawyer by day) and his band sometimes spill into this space to jam and even record.

A simple and inexpensive stairway guardrail composed of tongue-and-groove boards leads to the loft, which includes a couple of twin beds. The same boards make another appearance and add texture to the nearby closet doors.

   High windows to the north in the printmaking and painting studio invite indirect soft northern daylight while allowing for privacy and needed wall space for the wife's works to be displayed. The utilitarian, scored concrete slab floor suits the informality of the art studio.

# POOLSIDE ON THE BAY

ENGAGED WITH SITE    HUMAN SCALE    SIMPLE MASSING    SHELTERING ROOF    ECONOMY OF MEANS    INFORMALITY    SUNNY DISPOSITION    OPPOSITE COMPLEMENTS    CRAFTED DETAIL

**NESTLED AT THE BOTTOM OF A TERRACED LANDSCAPE** on the western end of the family pool, this cottage retreat in Jamestown, R.I., does everything the owners asked of it and then some. In the big picture, "I wanted it to be about the land and the property and the view," says the wife. Sited on the slightly expanded footprint of a failing greenhouse that it replaced, the cottage anchors the front corner of the pool area, overlooking the pool, past the main house (which also borders the pool), and ultimately out to Narragansett Bay.

*The exterior is traditional and contemporary at once.*

   Seen from the retained yard, with the pool and bay in the distance, the simple mass of the cottage's gabled form includes traditional shingle detailing and more contemporary oversized windows, doors, and transoms.

 The sheltering overhanging eaves help ground the pool cottage. Oversized door and adjacent window openings further reduce the scale of the building. A storage and mechanical closet is discreetly tucked into the white-clad bay to the left.

**Architect:** Gale Goff Architect
**Landscape architect:** Hali Beckman Ltd.
**Interiors:** Andrew Paraskos Interiors
Jamestown, R.I.
715 sq. ft.

The owners tasked architect Gale Goff with maximizing the small footprint to serve the pool and provide a hang-out space and spillover sleeping quarters for the family's three 20-something children and their friends. Gale was familiar with the property, having designed the main house for previous owners and a kitchen/family room addition for the current owners. Though the original main house was somewhat traditional, "The new client was more interested in being a little more modern, which was fun," explains Gale. The overhanging sheltering roof and simple gabled form of the pool cottage, clad in red cedar shingles with shingle flares at the gable ends and base like the main house, rings a traditional note. Yet the oversized windows and full-glass sliding doors suggest a more contemporary tone. As a result, the exterior is traditional and contemporary at once. Inside, the pendulum swings farther toward the contemporary.

Closest to the pool under a loft, Gale placed towel storage and laundry, the bathroom and its shower, as well as a kitchenette—all for easy access. Just beyond, the hang-out space opens with a taller ceiling and an expansive view of the front yard's stepped landscape and generous, retained side yard. The nearly 10-ft.-high flat ceiling of the compact service area complements the contrasting approximately 19½-ft. spacious cathedral ceiling in the adjacent sunny gathering room. The sleeping loft, accessed by alternating-tread stairs, adds a playful, informal touch—that is if the stairs don't scare you as they did the wife when she first descended it. She now advises those using it to turn and head down like you would a ladder. "I think it's a cool feature. It certainly is a conversation piece. Everybody talks about it," she notes.

Durability was of utmost importance to the owners, so they opted for porcelain-ceramic floor tiles throughout the main level over the concrete slab. They further determined that board finishes would hold up better than plaster, while also adding interesting texture. So, clean, horizontal boards with contemporary reveals wrap the walls and cover the ceiling, creating a calming, unifying, updated cottage effect. "I definitely wanted it to be minimalist. I didn't want a lot trim, a lot of curlicues, or anything like that," explains the wife.

When asked to name her favorite thing about the pool cottage retreat, the wife responds, "I love the fact that my kids love it." What more could you ask of a new cottage retreat?

The kitchenette's stone counters mesh nicely with the palette of 12-in. by 24-in. gray porcelain-ceramic floor tiles and pale yellow board-wall finish throughout. "I didn't want a lot of loud colors. I wanted everything to recede," explains the wife.

 The two-lite over two-lite double-hung windows recall the more traditional windows at the main house, but their size and grouping are much more current and also welcome abundant daylight. Gale dropped the windowsills nearly to the floor to increase visual access to the terraced garden. Stainless-steel tie rods above contribute to the airy, more contemporary interior.

 The pool and bay beyond are partly visible from the gathering room with its cathedral ceiling, which complements the contrasting lower ceiling in the entry service space below the loft. The crafted alternating-tread stairs that lead to the sleeping area under the sheltering roof takes up considerably less space than conventional stairs and amps up the fun.

# CREDITS

## IN A COMMUNITY

PHOTOGRAPHER: Randy O'Rourke
(pp. 146–147)

**SUMMER HEIRLOOM** (pp. 148–154)
ARCHITECT: Katie Hutchison Studio
www.katiehutchison.com
PHOTOGRAPHER: Tony Luong

**CAMPGROUND SALVAGE** (pp. 155–161)
HOMEOWNER DESIGNER: Kathryn Allen
PHOTOGRAPHERS: Randy O'Rourke
(pp. 159–161), Nat Rea (pp. 155–158)

**CAMPGROUND REDUX** (pp. vi bottom
left, 1, 146–147, 162–167)
HOMEOWNER DESIGNER: Erin Geddis
Cummings
PHOTOGRAPHERS: Randy O'Rourke,
p. 163 top courtesy of Erin Geddis
Cummings

**A SPEC WITH SIMPLICITY**
(pp. 168–173)
ARCHITECT: Estes Twombly Architects:
Jim Estes
www.estestwombly.com
PHOTOGRAPHER: Warren Jagger

**POCKET PATTERN** (pp. 132–139)
ARCHITECT: Ross Chapin Architects
www.rosschapin.com/
PHOTOGRAPHER: Amos Morgan

**FAMILY CAMP** (pp. 182–188)
HOMEOWNER ARCHITECT: Treacy &
Eagleburger Architects PC
www.treacyeagleburger.com
PHOTOGRAPHER: Randy O'Rourke

**ISLAND FOLK** (pp. 189–195)
ARCHITECT: LDa Architecture & Interiors:
Kyle Sheffield, Principal
www.lda-architects.com
PHOTOGRAPHER: Sean Litchfield

## RETREATS

**MARLBORO MUSIC COTTAGES**
(pp. 196–203)
ARCHITECT: HGA Architects and Engineers: Joan M. Soranno, Design Principal,
and John Cook, Senrio Project Architect
www.hga.com
PHOTOGRAPHER: Paul Crosby

**MINI SALT BOX** (pp. 204–207)
ARCHITECTURAL DESIGNER: FGS Design
LLC: Kiko Sanchez
INTERIORS: Lindroth Design: Amanda
Lindroth and Celine Lotmore
www.fgs-a.com
www.lindrothdesign.com
PHOTOGRAPHER: Carter Berg

**BACKYARD STUDIO** (pp. 208–211)
ARCHITECT: Estes Twombly Architects:
Peter Twombly
www.estestwombly.com
PHOTOGRAPHER: Warren Jagger

**POOLSIDE ON THE BAY** (pp. vi bottom
right, 212–215)
ARCHITECT: Gale Goff Architect
LANDSCAPE ARCHITECT: Hali Beckman
Ltd.
INTERIORS: Andrew Paraskos Interiors
www.galegoff.com
www.halibeckman.com
PHOTOGRAPHER: Anthony Crisafulli


**BACK COVER AUTHOR PHOTO**
PHOTOGRAPHER: Christopher Hufstader